The Angel Therapy® Handbook

Also by Doreen Virtue

Books/Kits/Oracle Board

Angel Words (with Grant Virtue)
Archangels 101
The Healing Miracles of Archangel Raphael
The Art of Raw Living Food (with Jenny Ross)
Signs from Above (with Charles Virtue)
The Miracles of Archangel Michael
Angel Numbers 101
Solomon's Angels (a novel)
My Guardian Angel (with Amy Oscar)
Angel Blessings Candle Kit (with Grant Virtue; includes booklet, CD, journal, etc.)
Thank You, Angels! (children's book with Kristina Tracy)
Healing Words from the Angels
How to Hear Your Angels
Realms of the Earth Angels
Fairies 101
Daily Guidance from Your Angels
Divine Magic
How to Give an Angel Card Reading Kit
Angels 101
Angel Guidance Board
Goddesses & Angels
Crystal Therapy (with Judith Lukomski)
Connecting with Your Angels Kit (includes booklet, CD, journal, etc.)
Angel Medicine
The Crystal Children
Archangels & Ascended Masters
Earth Angels
Messages from Your Angels
Angel Visions II
Eating in the Light (with Becky Prelitz, M.F.T., R.D.)
The Care and Feeding of Indigo Children
Healing with the Fairies
Angel Visions
Divine Prescriptions
Healing with the Angels
"I'd Change My Life If I Had More Time"
Divine Guidance
Chakra Clearing
Angel Therapy®
The Lightworker's Way
Constant Craving A–Z
Constant Craving
The Yo-Yo Diet Syndrome
Losing Your Pounds of Pain

Audio/CD Programs

Angel Therapy® Meditations
Archangels 101 (abridged audio book)
Fairies 101 (abridged audio book)
Goddesses & Angels (abridged audio book)
Angel Medicine (available as both 1- and 2-CD sets)
Angels among Us (with Michael Toms)
Messages from Your Angels (abridged audio book)
Past-Life Regression with the Angels
Divine Prescriptions
The Romance Angels
Connecting with Your Angels
Manifesting with the Angels
Karma Releasing
Healing Your Appetite, Healing Your Life
Healing with the Angels
Divine Guidance
Chakra Clearing

DVD Program

How to Give an Angel Card Reading

Oracle Cards (44 or 45 divination cards and guidebook)

Life Purpose Oracle Cards
Archangel Raphael Healing Oracle Cards
Archangel Michael Oracle Cards
Angel Therapy® Oracle Cards
Magical Messages from the Fairies Oracle Cards
Ascended Masters Oracle Cards
Daily Guidance from Your Angels Oracle Cards
Saints & Angels Oracle Cards
Magical Unicorns Oracle Cards
Goddess Guidance Oracle Cards
Archangel Oracle Cards
Magical Mermaids and Dolphins Oracle Cards
Messages from Your Angels Oracle Cards
Healing with the Fairies Oracle Cards
Healing with the Angels Oracle Cards

All of the above are available at your local bookstore, or may be ordered by visiting:
Hay House USA: **www.hayhouse.com®**; Hay House Australia: **www.hayhouse.com.au**;
Hay House UK: **www.hayhouse.co.uk**; Hay House South Africa: **www.hayhouse.co.za**;
Hay House India: **www.hayhouseco.in**

Doreen's Website: **www.AngelTherapy.com**

The Angel Therapy® Handbook

DOREEN VIRTUE

HAY HOUSE, INC.
Carlsbad, California • New York City
London • Sydney • Johannesburg
Vancouver • Hong Kong • New Delhi

Published and distributed in the United States by: Hay House, Inc.: www.hayhouse.com • ***Published and distributed in Australia by:*** Hay House Australia Pty. Ltd.: www.hayhouse.com.au • ***Published and distributed in the United Kingdom by:*** Hay House UK, Ltd.: www.hayhouse.co.uk • ***Published and distributed in the Republic of South Africa by:*** Hay House SA (Pty), Ltd.: www.hayhouse.co.za • ***Distributed in Canada by:*** Raincoast: www.raincoast.com • ***Published in India by:*** Hay House Publishers India: www.hayhouse.co.in

Editorial supervision: Jill Kramer • *Project editor:* Alex Freemon
Design: Jenny Richards

Library of Congress Cataloging-in-Publication Data

Virtue, Doreen.
The angel therapy handbook / Doreen Virtue. -- 1st ed.
p. cm.
ISBN 978-1-4019-1834-7 (hardcover : alk. paper) 1. Spiritual healing.
2. Angels--Miscellanea. I. Title.
BF1999.V50 2011
133.9--dc22 2010032457

Tradepaper ISBN: 978-1-4019-1836-1
Digital ISBN: 978-1-4019-2950-3

15 14 13 12 8 7 6 5
1st edition, January 2011
5th edition, January 2012

Printed in the United States of America

To God, Holy Spirit, Jesus,
the archangels, and the angels.

Contents

PART III: YOU ARE A SPIRITUAL TEACHER AND HEALER

Introduction

The Beginnings of Angel Therapy®*

As a child, I connected with angels whenever I felt lonely, sad, sick, or afraid. They appeared as dancing colored lights, similar to large Christmas-tree bulbs, which would gracefully move around me. I'd feel their presence as other-dimensional, and I'd hear beautiful otherworldly musical tones. The only thing I understood about angels was that they were comforting.

I was raised in a nontraditional Christian household where we combined the study of Jesus's healings described in the Bible with positive affirmations and visualizations. My parents used these tools for help with everyday living. For instance, when we needed a vehicle to replace our existing old clunker, they asked my brother and me to visualize that we had a new family car parked outside in the driveway. My dad even bought a small toy model of the one that he wished to manifest (which he covered in brown

*Angel Therapy, Angel Therapy Practitioner, ATP, Angel Intuitive, and Angel Therapist are internationally tradmarked terms. Only those who have been certified in Doreen Virtue's Angel Intuitive or Angel Therapy Practitioner courses are licensed to use these terms.

paint, because that was the color he wanted). Shortly thereafter, we *did* have that new brown car exactly as we'd visualized.

I remember my mother using prayer to heal our childhood illnesses and injuries. She'd also pray over our broken washing machine and car until they worked again. These prayers were solely directed to God and Jesus. Angels were only part of our vocabulary during Christmas and Valentine's Day, and even then they played minor roles.

The angels introduced themselves to me throughout my childhood. In addition to the comforting dancing-light visitations, I had vivid dreams that I recall to this day in which a wise man toured the world and other planets with me. My strongest memory was when the sage took me to a place that he called the equator and showed me a big river of bright fiery lava flowing through it.

Then when I was about six or seven years old, I was walking along the sidewalk in front of my family's church, on my way to attend Sunday school. Suddenly, the other-dimensional angel energy seemed to whoosh through my body. I felt myself fly high above the sidewalk, and I was shocked to look down upon myself! I saw my body standing still below me. Time seemed to stop momentarily, and a disembodied male voice asked me to observe myself. Then he said:

> *"This is your purpose, this separation of mind and body."*

Just as suddenly, I was back in my body, feeling confused as to what had just occurred.

Throughout my life, I had visitations from angels. I also clearly saw people who others said weren't there. I now know that I was mediumistic at a young age.

I was teased for being weird and different. A shy, sensitive child by nature, I rarely shared my odd experiences with others, in order to avoid additional ostracism.

I had lots of private conversations with my guides, though. As an example, when I spent too much time partying as a young adult, they clearly told me that I was wasting my life as if I were throwing it into a trash can. That had a big impact upon me and caused me to clean up my act. When I resumed drinking wine a few years later, I heard a voice clearly say to me, "Quit drinking and get into *A Course in Miracles!*" I followed this advice, to my benefit and pleasure.

During times of trouble, my guides would step in with lots of help. For instance, as a young mother, I struggled with finances. Yet each time I needed money for bills or food, it would magically appear. I'd either find $100 on the ground or I'd win contests, always in the nick of time to feed my family or pay the rent.

The angels helped me adjust my life so that I felt fairly healthy and happy. Still, I only told my closest family and friends about the visions and Divine guidance I received.

I put myself through college part-time, while working as an insurance secretary during the day and raising my two sons. It was a lot of hard work, but I felt guided to study psychology. So I persevered. Eventually, I graduated from Chapman University in Orange, California, with a B.A. and M.A. in counseling psychology. While going to college, I began volunteering at a CareUnit alcoholism and drug-abuse inpatient center in Palmdale, California. Eventually, the CareUnit hired me for a full-time counseling position.

I left the CareUnit to become a director at the Teen Alcohol and Drug Abuse Center (TADAC) in Lancaster, California. But since my passion was eating-disorder counseling, I eventually left TADAC to work under Dr. John Beck, a local psychiatrist. Dr. Beck helped me open an outpatient eating-disorders center called Victory Weight Management. There, I developed a successful practice

helping compulsive overeaters lose weight through counseling, visualization, and affirmations. I also gave my clients "readings," but didn't let them know that I was psychically receiving information for them.

I compiled my case studies into a book called *The Yo-Yo Diet Syndrome*, which my William Morris agent sold to HarperCollins Publishers. This set me on the busy path of giving media interviews and talks about eating disorders. Eventually, my tour schedule got so full that I no longer had time for my practice and the center. A therapist who worked with me took over the latter; and I spent my time writing, researching, and lecturing.

I continued authoring psychology books and articles about eating disorders and relationships. I also frequently appeared on TV and radio talk shows such as *Donahue, Geraldo, Ricki Lake,* and others of that genre. I traveled so much that the people at the LAX United Airlines ticket counter knew me by name when I'd walk up, which is remarkable considering they see thousands of customers daily.

Yet despite my apparent worldly success, inside I felt hollow. It seemed that I was missing the mark of my life purpose. Sure, I was helping people. But it wasn't "it." I worked at a couple more hospitals and clinics, but felt like a hamster running on a wheel who never could catch up with myself. I felt out of sorts, but unsure of what to do to feel better.

I thought that maybe a private practice would better suit my disposition. I left the clinics and hospitals, and began conducting my sessions over the telephone and in person. I did feel somewhat happier, but the emptiness persisted. I recognized the feeling as one of "existential angst," where you're searching for a sense of meaning and purpose . . . reassurance that what you're doing is meaningful.

I kept receiving the inner guidance to teach spiritual topics, which I resisted because of childhood memories of being teased

for being weird. So, I compromised by incorporating some spiritual principles into the books and articles I wrote. But generally, I kept up the appearance of "normalcy," while privately dealing with my increasingly anxious feelings that something was missing from my life.

Well, some people need to "hit bottom" in dramatic ways as a wake-up call to listening to their inner guidance. At that time in my life, I was one of those people! On July 15, 1995, I got *my* wake-up call, which forever changed my life.

I was getting dressed at my home in Newport Beach, California, when I heard a loud and clear male voice speaking into my right ear. It said: "You'd better put the top up on your car or it will be stolen."

I knew what the voice meant. My white 325i BMW automobile sat in the garage with its black cloth roof down, exposing the white upholstery of the interior. With its top down, the car was flashy and attention getting. But with its oxidized top up, no one looked twice at it.

I never second-guessed the voice's reality or thought it odd to have a conversation with a disembodied voice. Instead, I told the voice that the electric motor that controlled my car's top was broken. So I had no way of putting it up.

Instead of arguing back, the voice simply repeated itself: "You'd better put the top up on your car or it will be stolen." When I again told the voice that I couldn't pull the top up manually, it simply said, "Then have Grant do it."

I was stunned, and suddenly felt like I was in a fishbowl. The voice, the angel, knew that my then-14-year-old son Grant was in his bedroom at that moment. And truthfully, Grant probably could have dragged the top into the up position.

But the whole thing made me feel fidgety, and besides, I was running late for church. So I said good-bye to Grant and ran out of the house, saying silent prayers of protection along the way.

While driving to the church, I visualized my car surrounded by white light. I now know that this invocation is a way of asking the angels to protect you, since angels *are* intelligent and living beings of white light.

As I drove along Lincoln Boulevard in the city of Anaheim, I felt a heavy negative energy, as if someone had poured toxic paint over me and my car. My first thought was *I've been spotted!* exactly like prey in the gun sight of a hunter. I prayed harder as I pulled into the church parking lot.

I parked my car; grabbed my keys, purse, and a tape recorder I'd brought to record the church messages; and stood up. I then heard a loud male voice behind me scream expletives and demand my car keys and bag.

I turned to face a scowling man, pointing what looked like a gun at me. Behind him another man stood beside a car with its engine running.

I quickly noted that the man closest to me was significantly shorter than I was. His eyes were wide with fear. I intuitively knew that when he first spotted my car, he hadn't expected me to be so tall (I'm nearly 5'9" and wore high heels that day), and that he already felt anxious about what he was doing.

I also realized that if I gave him my keys as he was demanding, I'd suffer financially. You see, my car was fully paid for, so I only carried liability insurance. I didn't have any coverage to reimburse me for theft of the vehicle, so I was determined not to lose my automobile!

The voice of the angel who had spoken to me earlier returned. It said, "Scream with all of your might, Doreen!" This time, I didn't argue with it, and I screamed as loud as I could, with a sound emanating from deep in my belly. It felt primal, as if I'd accessed an inner cave woman. I watched the man's eyes grow wider as he backed away from me.

I thrust my tape recorder at him, and continued screaming

until a woman in the parking lot sitting in her car looked up and noticed the situation. She leaned on her horn to attract help, and hearing this, people ran out of the church. As the parking lot filled with witnesses, the men leapt into their getaway car and sped away.

I fell to my knees in shock and gratitude. I was still alive. I still had my car and my purse. My head spun as I realized that the disembodied voice had known, one hour before, that I would be threatened. How did it know this?

Kneeling in the parking lot, I profusely thanked God for protecting my life and my possessions. I felt humbled that I'd needlessly walked right into a life-endangering situation after ignoring the angel's warnings. I vowed to listen to my guidance from then on! My guidance was clear: teach as many people as possible, as quickly as possible, that the angels were real.

The next day, July 16, 1995, I was scheduled to give a brief talk and sign my book *Constant Craving* at a health-food convention in Las Vegas. Instead of wearing my then-typical business suit, I donned one of my favorite "goddess gowns" and wore a crystal necklace. I was ready to come out of the spiritual closet publicly and show who I really was!

I also began speaking about angels to the clients in my private practice and to the editors of my magazine articles. I told media producers that I could only appear on their television and radio shows if they'd let me talk about God and the angels. The producers of the Leeza Gibbons, *Donny & Marie,* Roseanne Barr, and *The View* shows agreed. Everyone else seemed to remove my name from their Rolodexes. Nonetheless, I stuck to my agreement and followed my guidance to teach about angels.

My clients seemed to move through their emotional issues rapidly with the help of the angels. A woman named Martha was particularly memorable: I'd been trying to help her (with traditional counseling) to overcome compulsive overeating for nearly a year. A Southern California elementary-school vice principal originally from Northern California, she was the first college graduate and administrator in her family, which was a real source of pride.

One day, Martha fell at work. Her doctor recommended back surgery, which she tried to delay due to fears about anesthesia and health repercussions. Martha tried chiropractic, massage, and Reiki to heal her back, but the pain continued, to the point where she was bedridden and could only walk with a cane.

After the attempted carjacking, I started to bring angels into my sessions with every client, and Martha was no exception. Days before her scheduled back surgery, I said to her, "If you could hear your angels talk to you about your back, what do you think they'd tell you?"

I'd already heard her angels' messages, but they had guided me to teach Martha how to hear them herself. They said to me, "If you tell her our message, she won't believe you. But if she hears it herself, she will believe and follow it."

Martha balked, and protested, "Oh, I don't think I can hear my angels!"

I was guided to gently coax her: "Martha, if you *could* hear your angels, what do you imagine that they'd say to you about your back?" The angels told me that couching the question as an imaginative venture would help Martha relax, even though the message would be quite real, *not* imaginary.

Martha sighed and whispered her reply: "I think they're saying that I'm in the wrong job, and I live too far away from my family."

Now it was my turn to sigh, because that was exactly what I'd also heard! I felt, heard, and saw the angels applauding both

Martha and me. I'd helped someone hear her angels!

The message was quite valid, as Martha had complained about the harsh political climate of the school where she worked. Yet, she was terrified of quitting, since everyone in her family was so proud of her career!

She obtained a release from her doctor, which allowed her to fly home for a visit. The minute she stepped off of the airplane, she was able to stand upright and walk without the cane, which she'd previously depended upon. Martha felt so good in the company of her family that she decided to look for work in the neighborhood.

She submitted a résumé to the local elementary school, and within two weeks, she was hired as the principal! This was a promotion over her previous vice-principal position. Martha happily accepted the job, canceled her surgery, and moved near her family. To this day, she's happier and healthier because she followed her angels' guidance.

Similar positive outcomes occurred with my other clients as we received and followed messages from their angels. I also received angelic instructions about healing methods, which yielded remarkable results for my clients and me.

I began writing about these angel messages and decided to ask my publisher, Hay House, if they were interested in publishing this material. Up until that time, I'd submitted lengthy proposals to formally ask the company to please consider a new book of mine. This time, I was guided to just send a one-paragraph e-mail description of the new book with the title *Angel Therapy.* Amazingly, Hay House's president, Reid Tracy, immediately agreed to publish the book, although neither he nor I knew what it would comprise.

As I was writing *Angel Therapy,* though, I experienced terrible headaches, which is a symptom I normally never have. As had become my new custom, I asked the angels for guidance. They told me that because I was channeling high-vibrating angelic

messages for the book, my low-vibrational diet was causing a clash of vibrations similar to a weather-system storm.

The angels showed me that my high consumption of chocolate every day was keeping my vibrations particularly low. They explained that my cravings for this substance were actually an indication of an appetite for love, but that I could only receive true love energetically and not through food.

I didn't know what to do, though, since I had daily cravings. So I appealed to the angels for help. Archangel Raphael, who is the angel of healing, appeared before me and held his stubby index finger between my eyes. I felt and saw bright green light waves being absorbed into my forehead. It was pleasant, like a very gentle massage.

The next day, I had no chocolate cravings. That was in 1996, and I haven't desired or eaten chocolate since. To me, this was a miracle, since I'd consumed it daily most of my life! (And P.S., my previously chronic acne cleared up as a result of my chocolate-free diet.)

Each time I learned a new angelic healing method, I'd use it to help my clients. Although I'd once feared public ostracism for so openly speaking about angels, the reverse happened and my schedule became jam-packed with clients and speaking opportunities. My reading calendar got booked up nearly three years in advance! I realized that unless I took control of my schedule, my calendar would become progressively filled—indefinitely into the future.

So I went for a walk to the beach and prayed about the situation. I turned everything over to God and said, "I trust that You know the perfect solution to balancing my schedule." I immediately got a vision, and the knowingness of what to do: I was to start teaching *other* people how to conduct angel readings and therapy.

My courses were originally called Certified Spiritual Counselor workshops, and then later I changed the name to Angel Therapy Practitioner® workshops. I also initiated a modified program called Angel Intuitive®, which I only teach in Australia.

So, this is a handbook covering the methods and messages that I teach in my courses. Some of the material in these pages is extracted from my other works in an effort to make sure that this is a thorough overview of Angel Therapy. My prayer is that this book will be a resource to awaken you to your clear connection with the Divine and lead you upon the path of your life purpose.

With love,

Doreen Virtue

PART I

Connecting with the Angels and Archangels

CHAPTER 1

The Angels

Before we dive into the study of Angel Therapy, let's define our terms and create a foundation of core knowledge about the angels.

An "angel," in our terms, is a celestial (nonphysical) being who is an egoless messenger of God. In fact, the word *angel* derives from the Greek and translates to the phrase "messenger of God." Angels are the deliverers of Heaven's love and guidance.

Speaking as a lifelong clairvoyant, I've seen that every person has at least two guardian angels. Many people have more, either because they've asked for additional angels or because others have asked God to send them on their behalf. These are your personal angels, who are with you for your entire lifetime. Some angels will come and go throughout your life, depending upon your circumstances and needs. But your core guardian angels will remain consistent.

Your guardian angels are with you every moment of every day. They unconditionally love you, no matter what, and want the

best for you. They never tire of you or get bored, frustrated, or upset with you. They're angels, after all!

Help from the Angels

We don't pray to, or worship, the angels. We give all glory to God. The angels are nondenominational and assist people of every belief. They work alongside Jesus and the ascended masters of all religious faiths.

The angels have a purpose to enact God's will, which is peace upon Earth, one person at a time. These beings know that if *each* of us is peaceful, then we'll have a *world* of peaceful people. So, really, your life's purpose is to be at peace, and the angels want to help you with this.

While it's true that challenges do help us grow, the angels also say that serenity leads to even bigger growth spurts. Through tranquility, our schedules and creativity are more open to giving service, and our bodies operate in a healthy fashion. Our relationships thrive and blossom, and we're shining examples of God's love.

Sometimes people say to me, "Well, God already knows what I need, so I won't ask for anything." True . . . however, we were created with free will. This means that God and the angels can't intervene into our lives without our permission. In other words, we must ask for their help before they can assist us.

It doesn't matter *how* you ask, but only that you *do.* You can say your request aloud, silently, or in writing. You can sing, whisper, type, or even scream your request for Heaven's guidance. You can word it in positive, affirmative ways or as an appeal of supplication. Any form of asking for assistance is enough to give God and the angels permission to intervene.

I also hear people say, "I don't want to bother Heaven with my petty tasks." To celestial beings, though, nothing is too small

or too large. They simply want to help us with whatever brings us peace, and many times it's the small favors that result in long-lasting peacefulness. The angels say that it's also the small stressors in life that erode peace. So ask for help, as your contribution to world peace.

If you don't know what to ask for, that's okay. You can simply say, "Please help me to be at peace," and they'll get to work on your behalf. Or request something specific and say, "This, or something better, please, God," since Heaven always has higher standards than our own.

Just don't hand God and the angels a script about how to fix a situation. Similarly, don't waste time or energy worrying about how Heaven will help you. The "how" is up to God's infinite Divine wisdom. Your job is only to ask for help and then to follow the guidance sent to you (more on this guidance later).

I'm sometimes asked, "Why should I talk to angels when I can talk to God?" This is an excellent question! When I posed it to God and the angels, here's the reply I received:

"When people are afraid and most in need of Heavenly help, their vibrations are too low to hear and feel the pure love of God. The angels, who are closer to Earth, are easier to hear and feel when someone is fearful or stressed. Then they can lift the person's vibrations and help him or her be unafraid and at peace and return to a clear connection with God."

Everyone can hear and talk with God and the angels. You don't need to be specially trained, qualified, or deserving. *All* are equally qualified and deserving of Heaven's love and help. You were created in the image and likeness of God. So you share the Divine qualities of love, abundance, health, beauty, and goodness. We all do.

You might ask, "Since everyone has guardian angels, why is

there evil and suffering in the world?" Another excellent question. If everyone listened to their guardian angels, we'd have a world of loving and peaceful people. There would be no evil, which stems from fear about a lack of resources, which in turn causes people to act selfishly.

When you work with angels, in contrast, you begin to understand that there is no need to compete, because there is plenty of everything to go around for everyone. You begin to share freely, without fear of running out of resources.

Angels are different from departed friends and relatives. While these people can act like angels, they're still humans with egos and fallible opinions. There's no problem with talking with your grandma or other departed loved ones to keep in contact. To get pure Divine guidance, though, you'll want to direct your conversations to God and the egoless angels (and Jesus or other ascended masters with whom you feel aligned). (In Chapter 3, we'll focus on mediumship, which is the art of connecting with loved ones in Heaven on behalf of yourself and others.)

The spirit world, where angels live, isn't a faraway place. Heaven is all around us, in a different dimension. This is similar to the frequency bands of different radio stations all existing simultaneously.

Your angels are celestial beings who have not lived on the earth before as humans, unless they were previously *incarnated angels,* who manifest into human form either temporarily to avert a crisis, or for an entire lifetime so that they can more directly help and guide people.

The Nine Choirs of Angels

Angelology, the study of angels, holds that there are nine "choirs" or branches of angels, which include:

- **Seraphim**: These are the highest order of angels, who are said to be shining bright, as they are closest to God. They are pure light.

- **Cherubim**: Usually portrayed as chubby children with wings à la Cupid, the Cherubim are the second-highest order. They are pure love.

- **Thrones**: The triad of Seraphim, Cherubim, and Thrones resides in the highest realms of Heaven. Thrones are the bridge between the material and the spiritual, and represent God's fairness and justice.

- **Dominions**: The Dominions are the highest in the next triad level of angels. They are the overseers or managers of angels, according to God's will.

- **Virtues**: These angels govern the order of the physical universe, watching over the sun, the moon, the stars, and all of the planets, including Earth.

- **Powers**: As their name implies, Powers are peaceful warriors who purify the universe from lower energies.

- **Principalities**: The third triad consists of the angels closest to Earth. The Principalities watch over the planet, including nations and cities, to ensure God's will of peace on Earth.

- **Archangels**: This choir comprises the overseers of humankind and of the guardian angels. Each archangel has a specialty representing an aspect of God.

- **Guardian angels**: Each individual has personal guardian angels assigned to him or her throughout life.

This model of nine choirs dates from the biblical references to Seraphim and Cherubim, and was expanded in the 5th-century writings of Pseudo-Dionysius and then popularized in John Milton's poetic work *Paradise Lost*.

Calling All Angels

You can call additional celestial helpers to your side, since there are countless angels. To do so, you may either mentally or verbally ask God to send them to you, directly ask them to come to you, or visualize more of them with you. Any method works, as long as you ask. As stated earlier, don't worry that you're bothering the angels with your requests. They're unlimited beings who are glad to help bring you peace.

Like people, angels have specialties. You can ask for the ones best qualified to help with a particular situation, or call upon the following specialty angels:

- **Angels of abundance:** These angels guide you in making wise financial decisions, give career boosts, bring about financial windfalls, help you meet your basic needs, leave coins for you to find, and help with Divine timing in career moves.

- **Healing angels:** Led by the archangel Raphael, these angels surround ailing people with healing energy, calm worries about health, guide your decisions about medical care, help aspiring or current healers, and release negativity, such as anger or pessimism.

- **Moving angels:** These angels guide you to find the perfect new home, help you sell or rent your previous home, assist with financing and qualifying for a new residence, ease the relocation process, keep moving-related stress to a minimum, and protect your belongings during the move.
- **Romance angels:** These cherubic angels bring people together, heal troubled relationships (and add fun and passion to them), and offer guidance about readying yourself to meet your soul mate.
- **Fitness angels:** Fitness angels boost your motivation to get—and keep—your body physically fit, guide you to the right form of exercise, reduce or eliminate cravings, help you choose healthful foods and beverages, and keep you from feeling deprived or making excuses.
- **Nature angels:** Also known as devas, fairies, and elementals, these special angels are guardians of plants, bodies of water, and domestic and wild animals. They assist you with gardening, or attracting birds and butterflies to your garden; guide you to make ecologically sound choices; urge you to pick up trash during outdoor walks; and help those who wish to adopt a vegetarian or vegan lifestyle.
- **Driving and parking angels:** These powerful angels help you find your destination, arrive on time, and find a parking space. (Mentally ask for a spot before you reach your destination to allow the angels time to arrange a great opening for you.)

- **Beauty angels:** Led by the archangel of beauty, Jophiel, these angels help you choose the best outfit, hairstyle, and accessories for any situation; guide you to wonderful hairdressers; assist you in plucking stubborn chin hairs; bring you gifts; make you glow from the inside; and show you how very attractive you are!

- **Family angels:** These loving angels, led by the archangels Gabriel and Metatron, help you with all aspects of child rearing, including adoption and conception; assist with domestic projects and decisions; maintain family unity and peace; encourage family members to be open-minded and compassionate toward one another; and protect the home.

- **Warrior angels:** These angels, championed by the archangel Michael, peacefully and lovingly fight on behalf of underdogs and social issues, help grassroots causes, assist charitable organizations, protect children and guard against domestic violence, safeguard your home and valuables, give courage and outlets to those who wish to speak or write about injustices, and aid pro bono lawyers.

Angels *do* have gender energies that make them look and act distinctively masculine or feminine. However, each of us has a team of Divine companions with a different ratio of males to females. So you might have three males and one female, while your sister has two females.

All angels really do have wings and a Heavenly appearance, similar to the look of Renaissance paintings reproduced on holiday cards and in religious art. They don't use these wings for transportation in my experience, as I've never seen an angel "flapping." I've seen them enfold a person in their wings for comfort, and that's the sole purpose served, from what I've seen.

One time the angels told me that the only reason they have wings is due to our Western expectations. They said:

"The original painters of angels mistook our aura of light for wings, so they depicted us with wings in their paintings, and we appear to you this way so that you will know that it is us, your angels."

Your Guardian Angels' Names

Just like people, all angels have names. Your personal relationship with *your* guardian angels will deepen as you speak with them regularly. One way to get to know them even better is to ask them to identify themselves.

In a quiet moment without distractions, think or vocalize the request: "Angels, please tell me your names," and then notice the name that comes to you as a thought, word, feeling, or vision. It's best to write these impressions down so you'll remember them.

Some of the names may sound unusual. If you don't receive any at all, it usually means that you're trying too hard to hear. Wait until a time when you're relaxed and ask again.

Next, say to your angels: "Please send me signs in the physical world that I'll easily notice to help me validate that I've heard your names correctly." You'll then encounter the names that you've received by way of people you meet, conversations you overhear, and so forth.

You can do this for others, too, even if you're not physically with the person for whom you're receiving angel names. Just tune in to the individual, relax your shoulders, breathe deeply, hold the intention of connecting with his or her angels, and follow the same guidelines outlined above.

Usually, our lower self (the ego) argues that we're making these names up. That's why we ask the angels to send physical signs to validate that we've heard them accurately.

You'll be amazed by the creative ways in which the angels will help confirm that you've heard correctly!

Next, we'll focus upon the archangels, who watch over our guardian angels and each and every person on Earth.

CHAPTER 2

The Archangels

Archangels are the managers of the angels. They are one of the nine choirs of angels listed in the previous chapter. Of all these Heavenly beings, the guardian angels and archangels are the most involved with helping Earth and her inhabitants.

Archangels are larger and more powerful than angels. They're nonphysical . . . yet they're very much perceptible, audible, and visible as you tune in to them. As celestial beings, they don't have genders. However, their specific fortes and characteristics give them distinct male and female energies and personas.

The word *archangel* is derived from the Greek *archi,* which means "first, principal, or chief"; and *angelos,* which means "messenger of God." So, archangels are the chief messengers of God.

Archangels are extremely powerful celestial beings. Each one has a specialty, and represents an aspect of God. You can think of them as facets on the face of God, the ultimate jewel and gem of the universe. These facets, or archangels, are prisms that radiate Divine light and love in specific ways to everyone on Earth.

Artwork portrays archangels as ideal human forms with large eagle- or swanlike wings, in contrast to artistic depictions of Cherubim (cherubs) as babies with small wings.

The archangels are among God's original creations, and they existed long before humankind or organized religions. They belong to God, not to any specific theology. Therefore, archangels work with people of all different beliefs and paths. In fact, they work with whoever asks.

Just like guardian angels, the archangels are nondenominational, and they help anyone, regardless of the person's religious or nonreligious background. They're able to be with each one of us, individually and simultaneously, because they're beyond space and time restrictions. Imagine what our lives would be like if we could be in different places at once! Well, the angels say that the only reason we don't experience bilocality is because we *believe* that we can only be in one location at a time. Soon, we'll learn how to lift that restriction, according to them.

The reason why I emphasize this point is that some people worry that if they call upon Archangel Michael, for example, they might be pulling him away from a more "important" assignment. This is how we project our human limitations! The fact is that the archangels and ascended masters can be with anyone who desires their assistance, and have a unique experience with each being. So know that you can call upon the archangels by mentally asking them to help you. No formal prayers are necessary.

Identifying the Archangels

The exact number of archangels who exist depends upon which belief system or spiritual text you consult. The Bible, the Qur'an, the Testament of Levi, the Kabbalah, the Third Book of

Enoch, and the writings of Pseudo-Dionysius all list and describe differing numbers and names.

Suffice it to say that there are many archangels, although I usually only highlight Michael, Raphael, Gabriel, and Uriel in my books and workshops. However, lately the others have been urging me to involve them in my life and work, so here are some additional descriptions of archangels and how you may wish to work with them. The different gender designations come from my interactions with these beings. Since angels and archangels don't have physical bodies, their gender relates to the energy of their specialties. For example, Archangel Michael's strong protectiveness is very male, while Jophiel's focus upon beauty is very female.

— **Archangel Ariel**'s name means "lion or lioness of God." Known as the archangel of the earth, she works tirelessly on behalf of the planet. She oversees the elemental kingdom and helps in the healing of animals, especially the nondomesticated kind. Call upon Ariel to become better acquainted with the fairies, to help with environmental concerns, or to heal an injured wild bird or other animal.

— **Archangel Azrael**'s name means "whom God helps." Azrael is sometimes called the Angel of Death because he meets people at the time of their physical passing and escorts them to the Other Side. He helps newly crossed-over souls feel comfortable and very loved. This archangel assists ministers of all religions and also spiritual teachers. Call upon Azrael for your deceased or dying loved ones, and also for help with your formal or informal ministry.

Because of their similar-sounding names, Azrael is sometimes confused with Azazael, who is considered a fallen angel. Yet their personas, missions, and energies couldn't be more different. Our Azrael is a pure and trustworthy being of God's light.

— **Archangel Chamuel**'s name means "he who sees God." He helps us locate important parts of our lives. Call upon Chamuel to find a new love interest, new friendships, a different job, or any lost item. Once found, your new situation can be maintained and developed with the help of this archangel. So ask him if you need assistance in repairing any misunderstandings in personal or work relationships.

— **Archangel Gabriel**'s name means "God is my strength." In early Renaissance paintings, Gabriel is portrayed as a female archangel, although later writings refer to this being with masculine pronouns (perhaps because of the Council of Nicaea's massive editing of scriptures). She's the messenger angel who helps all earthly messengers such as writers, teachers, and journalists. Call upon Gabriel to overcome fear or procrastination in any endeavor involving communication or any aspect of child conception, adoption, pregnancy, and early childhood.

— **Archangel Haniel**'s name means "grace of God." Call upon this angel whenever you wish to add grace and its effects (peace, serenity, enjoyment of good friends' company, beauty, harmony, and so on) to your life. You can also request aid before any event in which you desire to be the embodiment of grace, such as giving an important presentation, being interviewed for a job, or going on a first date.

— **Archangel Jeremiel**'s name means "mercy of God." He's an inspirer who motivates us to devote ourselves to spiritual acts of service. He's also involved with the process of attaining Divine wisdom. Call upon Jeremiel if you feel "stuck" spiritually so that you may regain enthusiasm about your path and Divine mission. This archangel provides comfort for emotional healing, and is wonderfully helpful with forgiveness issues.

— **Archangel Jophiel**'s name means "beauty of God." She's the patron archangel of artists, and helps us see and maintain beauty in life. Call upon her before beginning any artistic project. Since Jophiel is involved in beautifying the planet by cleansing it of pollution, you can also ask her for assignments to help in this vital mission. I sometimes refer to Jophiel as the "feng shui" angel, because she can help you clear out clutter from your office, your home, or even your life in general.

— **Archangel Metatron**'s name means "angel of the Presence." He's thought to be the youngest and the tallest of the archangels, and one of the two who once walked upon the earth as a man (as the prophet Enoch). Metatron works with Mother Mary to help children, both living and crossed over. In the Kabbalah, Metatron is the chief angel of the Tree of Life, where he guides humans at the start of their spiritual journey. Call upon him for any kind of assistance you may need with your little ones. His intervention often involves helping youngsters open their spiritual awareness and understanding. He also assists Crystal and Indigo children in keeping their spiritual gifts awakened and coping with school and other aspects of life.

— **Archangel Michael**'s name means "he who is as God" or "he who looks like God." He's the archangel who releases the effects of fear from the planet and its inhabitants. The patron of police officers, he gives all of us the courage and backbone to follow our truth and fulfill our Divine mission. Call upon Michael if you feel afraid or confused about your personal safety, your Heavenly purpose, or making a necessary life change. You can also ask him to help you fix any mechanical or electrical problems. In addition, Michael can assist you in remembering your life purpose, and then give you the courage to follow through on it.

— **Archangel Raguel**'s name means "friend of God." He's often called the archangel of justice and is the champion of underdogs. Ask him for aid whenever you feel that you're being overpowered or manipulated. Raguel will intervene by giving you guidance about how to attain balanced power and fairness within the structure of your personal and community relationships. Also call upon him on behalf of another person who's being treated unfairly. Raguel will help you harmonize all of your relationships.

— **Archangel Raphael**'s name means "God heals," and he's in charge of physical healings. He helps all those dedicated to the promotion of health and wellness; this extends to those who are not yet active in this field. Call upon Raphael to heal any injuries or illnesses you or others (including animals) are suffering with. Ask him to help with your healing work, including education and building a private practice. In addition, Archangel Raphael aids those who are traveling, so request that he ensure a harmonious and safe journey.

— **Archangel Raziel**'s name means "secret of God." He is said to stand very near to God, so he hears all Divine conversations about universal secrets and mysteries. He wrote these secrets in a document that he gave to Adam, which eventually ended up in the hands of the prophets Enoch and Samuel. Call upon Raziel whenever you wish to understand esoteric material (including your dreams) or to engage in alchemy, past-life, or manifestation work.

— **Archangel Sandalphon**'s name means "brother," because, like Archangel Metatron, he was once a human prophet (Elijah) who ascended into archangeldom. Sandalphon is the archangel of music and answered prayers. He helps Archangel Michael clear away fear and the effects of fear (with music). Put on a soothing CD and call upon him to dispel any spiritual confusion.

— **Archangel Uriel**'s name means "God is light." This Heavenly being pours light upon a troubling situation, which illuminates your problem-solving abilities. Call upon Uriel whenever you get into a sticky situation and you need to think clearly and find answers. Uriel also helps students and those who need intellectual assistance.

— **Archangel Zadkiel**'s name means "righteousness of God." He has long been regarded as the angel of good memory, and like Uriel, he's a great helper of students. Call upon Zadkiel to help you remember *anything,* including your own divinity.

In Angel Therapy, we primarily work with Archangel Michael to cut etheric cords (more on this later) and clear and shield our bodies and energy fields, and with Raphael to help with all aspects of healing.

Interacting with Archangels

Since archangels are so close to Earth and humankind, it's natural for us to connect with them. In fact, the Bible is filled with accounts of people interacting with Michael and Gabriel. The archangels seek to work with us in conjunction with God's will.

We don't pray to archangels, nor do we worship them. As I said in the last chapter, all glory goes to God. We work with archangels simply because they are God's intended gift to us all, and part of the Divine plan for peace.

So why don't we simply direct all questions and requests to God? As I mentioned, the archangels are extensions of God who are easier to hear and feel during times of great stress. Their vibrations are very condensed, and they're palpable and practically tangible. Just as looking at a sunset or a rainbow reminds us of God's love, so do the archangels.

We don't need to be saintly or perfectly behaved to elicit the archangels' help. They look past human mistakes and see the inner goodness within us all. They want to bring peace to Earth by helping us *all* to be peaceful. So their mission includes assisting the "unpeaceful" people of the world.

The archangels are unlimited beings, as holograms of God's omnipresence. Remember the promise that Jesus made: "I am with you always"? Well, the archangels—like Jesus—are able to be with each person who calls upon them.

The key is that the archangels will never violate our free will by intervening without permission, even if to do so would make us happier. They must wait until we give our consent in some way: a prayer, a cry for help, a wish, visualization, affirmations, or a thought.

You needn't worry about asking for the archangels help incorrectly. You don't have to be specially trained or use fancy invocations to garner their attention. Any sincere call for help is enough, as all they need is your permission.

Affirmative and supplicant prayers work. In the former, it's a positive here-and-now statement or visualization, such as "Thank you, Archangel Michael, for protecting me," and in the latter it's an appeal, like "Please protect me, Archangel Michael." Both yield the identical results.

Same with the questions "Should I call upon God directly? Should I ask God to send the appropriate angels? Or should I appeal to the angels themselves?" These questions imply that there's a separation between God and the angels, which there's not.

The more you work with the archangels, the more you'll begin to trust them. You'll feel peaceful, knowing for certain that you're safe and protected in all situations.

The Archangels in Sacred Texts

The archangels have been described and accounted for in spiritual texts such as:

— **The Bible.** Michael and Gabriel are the only two archangels specifically named in the Bible. The Book of Daniel describes them both, including Gabriel's role in helping Daniel interpret his visions, along with a mention of Michael as "one of the chief princes." In Luke, Gabriel famously announces the forthcoming births of John the Baptist and Jesus Christ. Michael also appears in the Book of Jude, protecting Moses's body, and in Revelations.

— **Apocryphal and Talmudic biblical books.** The scriptural texts that aren't in the canonical Bible are still regarded as sacred, and are part of the Bible of the Eastern Orthodox and other churches. The Book of Enoch discusses the archangels Michael, Raguel, Gabriel, Uriel, and Metatron. The Book of Tobit is the account of Archangel Raphael leading Tobias's travels and helping him create healing ointments for his father, Tobit. The Book of 2 Esdras (recognized by the Coptic church) refers to Archangel Uriel, calling him the "angel of salvation."

— **The Qur'an.** The Islamic scripture was revealed to Muhammad by Gabriel (Jibrayil). The Qur'an and Muslim tradition also describe archangels Michael (Mikaaiyl), Raphael (Israfil), and Azrael (Izrael).

How Many Archangels Are There?

The answer depends upon whom you ask. Traditionally, people think of the four archangels Michael, Raphael, Gabriel, and Uriel. However, as I mentioned, only two are named in the traditional Bible.

The Bible's Book of Revelation tells us that there are seven archangels, and in the noncanonical Book of Tobit, Raphael says he is one of seven. The Gnostics also held seven archangels in esteem. Historians believe that the sacredness of the number seven comes from the Babylonians' blend of religion and astronomy, with reverence for the seven planets' mystical powers.

Which seven archangels make this list, though, differs from source to source. And that's not even taking into account that each archangel's name has alternative spellings and pronunciations.

In the mystical Kabbalah, ten archangels represent each of the *Sephiroth,* or aspects of God. Metatron is the chief archangel in this Judaic tradition.

So the topic of how many archangels exist can be confusing and subjective. I tried to answer this question to my own satisfaction while researching and writing my book *Archangels & Ascended Masters*. My methodology was to learn as much as I could about the archangels, and then have personal interactions and connections with each one. The 15 archangels whom I was easily able to reach and research, and who emanated God's pure love and light, are the ones I work with.

In truth, there are legions of archangels helping us here on Earth. In fact, Eastern Orthodox theology holds that there are thousands. My prayer is that we will be open-minded and welcome trustworthy archangels into our sphere of spiritual friends.

If you're concerned about lower energies, I want to reassure you that there's no way that any fear-based physical or spiritual being could mimic the profound, warm healing love and light

that emanate from our beloved archangels of God. Plus, if you ask God, Jesus, and Archangel Michael to shield you from lower energies, they're happy to ensure that only beings of light are with you.

Yes, there *are* lower-energy, fear-based spiritual beings whom some call "angels" but who are actually Earthbound spirits. For example, an "archangel" named Samael was once called the "Angel of Light" or the "Lightbearer." But then Samael's light fell, and he became vengeful and dark. This seems to be the basis of the ideology about Lucifer, which isn't specifically mentioned in the Bible but is discussed through mythology and legend.

I stay far away from these dark "angels" of occultists, including those supposedly associated with King Solomon. The occult legend holds that Solomon used his magical ring embossed with the Star of David to control demons who built his Temple. The names of these 72 demons are sometimes presented as a list of angel names, but they're not angels. These teachings, the so-called Solomonic Lesser and Greater Keys, bring in dark and untrustworthy energy. (By the way, I don't believe that the good King Solomon worked with lower energies.)

Some occultists invoke the names of the sacred archangels Michael, Raphael, Gabriel, and Uriel in fear-based ceremonies. My advice: Stay away from any religion or spiritual practice that is fear or guilt based. Stick with the real angels of God's light and love—they're the ones who will really bring you the peace and happiness you desire.

The main response I hear from those who begin working with archangels is: "This changed my life for the better!" People become happier, healthier, and more peaceful and sure-footed as a result of doing so. The archangels are a very personal way to connect with God's love and wisdom.

Aura Colors, Crystals, and Astrological Signs of the Archangels

Every archangel has a specific purpose, which results in different vibrations that can be viewed as distinct energy or aura emanations. Sometimes you'll detect the archangels' presence as sparkling or flashing colored lights (much like I did as a child). In the Appendix of this book, I've listed the colors, gemstones, and astrological signs associated with the various archangels.

The archangels work with anyone who calls upon them, and they have important functions in Angel Therapy healing and divination work. During many sessions, departed loved ones also come through with loving messages, which is a topic we'll explore in the next chapter.

CHAPTER 3

Departed Loved Ones and Mediumship

If you ask 100 people the question "What is an angel?" probably half will answer that it's a beloved relative or friend in Heaven. The other half will describe a traditional winged celestial being.

Well, technically, angels refer to messengers of God. And while your dear departed grandma may be saintlike, chances are that she still has a human ego. Your deceased loved ones exist in the spirit world, but they function at an energy frequency that's different from your angels. So, as angelic as some of them are, they're really more "spirit guides" than angels. Still, it's part of personal and professional healing to learn how to contact them, in a process known as *mediumship*.

You can definitely contact your crossed-over friends and family members. I recommend doing so if you have unfinished business with them, such as unresolved feelings of anger, or if you

worry about their degree of happiness. You can certainly get advice from a deceased loved one; however, take it with the same healthy skepticism you'd employ when being advised by a living person.

Remember: People don't become saints or psychics just because they've passed on. They may have more patience and more insight from the perspective of the spirit plane, but they're still Uncle Fred and Aunt Harriet, meaning that they retain their earthly personalities and quirks. And while they're happy to help you, especially when it comes to topics related to their earthly specialty (for example, if Uncle Fred was a banker, he'll gladly give you financial guidance), it's best to consult the Creator and the angels for trustworthy advice about major issues in life.

You can also get in touch with departed loved ones who didn't have the ability to speak your language at the time of their death. In other words, unborn children; babies; and those who were mute, spoke a foreign language, or were otherwise unable to communicate can converse with you in the universal language of feelings, through visions, or in other nonverbal ways.

Don't worry that you're bothering your deceased loved ones if you contact them. People in the spirit world, like those on Earth, have free will. If they're busy, they'll send a message through the ethers or through another departed loved one. Truly, the only thing that holds back deceased loved ones is any unhealed grief on your part. They welcome the opportunity to deliver the healing message that they love you and are doing well in the afterlife.

It's normal to grieve heavily for about six months following a loss, but then gradually the depression and anger wear away. However, some mourning people put their lives on hold for years. I've met individuals who were suicidal, addicted to sleeping pills, or housebound due to their unrelenting grief. This behavior can block departed loved ones from their spiritual growth. The greatest favor you can do for someone who has passed away is to heal

your heart of grief. Ways to do that include joining a support group, connecting with him or her to reassure yourself that all is well, journaling, and taking excellent care of your body.

Conducting Mediumship for Yourself

If you've lost people whom you were close to, chances are they've spent time with you after they crossed over, and they may even be with you on a regular basis. After all, in addition to angels, archangels, and ascended masters, you also have deceased loved ones with you to help. They may be relatives who passed before your birth, people with whom you shared a close bond, or those from your past who can teach you a special skill for your life's purpose.

When people leave this plane, they're eventually given the option of performing service work, both to expand their own spiritual progress and to help others. Some volunteer to become guides to their living loved ones. They usually elect to stay until the end of their charges' physical lives. Time measurement is different in Heaven, so if you live to be 95, it feels like a much shorter period to those on the Other Side.

These beings are with you because they care about you. In addition, you may have a similar mission—that is, being with you is a way for the deceased loved ones who are by your side to vicariously fulfill their life purpose if they didn't do so while in their earthly bodies. If you were named after your dear departed Aunt Suzanne, chances are she's your spirit guide. Namesakes nearly always stay with you. Perhaps you were given that name because your parents intuitively realized your soul-path similarities.

So, when Aunt Suzanne decides to be your spirit guide, she first must go through the equivalent of a spiritual-counselor training program. In that Heavenly school, she learns how to be with you in a supportive way without interfering with your free will,

as well as how to travel the astral plane and still be within earshot should you ever call for help. She finds out how to communicate with you through your strongest spiritual-communication channel, such as your dreams, inner voice, gut feelings, or intellectual insights. It takes time to train to become a spirit guide. That's why recently deceased loved ones aren't with you continuously. Only someone who has gone through extensive training can be by your side night and day.

Let's say that Aunt Suzanne was a very successful newspaper reporter and you're an aspiring author. In fact, writing is part of your life's purpose. So when you ask Heaven, "What's my mission in life?" your aunt telepathically encourages you to write. Of course, she's only doing this because she knows what God's Divine mission is for you.

Sometimes people will ask me if it's okay to talk with those on the Other Side. They may quote from the Torah, which cautions against speaking to the dead and mediums. I can understand these warnings, because it's a mistake to turn our lives over to those who have passed on, just as it isn't right to give control to those who are living.

We want our higher selves, in conjunction with our Creator, to be in charge. Our deceased loved ones can definitely help us, but as I mentioned, they're not automatically saints, angels, or psychics just because their souls have crossed over. However, they can work in concert with God, the Holy Spirit, the ascended masters, and the angels to help us fulfill Divine will (which is in alignment with the higher self's intentions). I think the main reason to contact these guides is for that extra boost of help they can provide, as well as to maintain or deepen our relationships with them.

I'm also asked whether we're bothering departed loved ones when we call upon them. Just as living people have the option to say *no* when they don't want to be disturbed, so do the spirits in Heaven. My experience, though, is that departed people love to be helpful. After all, they have all the time in the "other world" now! And mostly, they want to help because they love you.

For Those Who Are Adopted

I'm often asked about the spirit guides of adoptees. I've found that these individuals have more angels and deceased loved ones with them than others do. Adopted people always have a spirit guide who's a relative from their birth family—I've never seen an exception to this. It could be a parent, sibling, grandparent, aunt, or uncle who has passed away. It doesn't matter whether the adopted person ever met this family member or not. The bond is there, regardless of whether a relationship was forged while both parties were simultaneously living.

In addition, these folks have guides from the friends and adopted family members whom they've been with along the way. I believe that they have more angels than those who weren't adopted, to protect them and help them adjust to the life changes that result from the process of adoption.

Deepening Your Relationship with Deceased Loved Ones

"Are my departed loved ones okay?" is a question I hear continually. The reason people ask is simple: the fear that someone is in some sort of "hellish" place, literally or figuratively. Yet my readings find that nearly all deceased people are doing just fine, thank you. Their only discomfort has to do with you and me, especially if we're grief stricken to the point of obsession or emotional paralysis. They're going on with their lives, and they want us to do the same. If we hold back our spiritual progress or happiness due to grief, those who have passed on are held back in similar ways.

In fact, it's safe to say that the only problem most people in Heaven have is . . . *us!* If we'd go on to live happy, productive lives, our deceased loved ones would sing and rejoice in jubilant celebration.

On the Other Side, spirits feel wonderful physically. All illness, injury, and disability disappear once the body is gone. The soul is intact and in perfect health. Everyone still feels like him- or herself, but without the heaviness and pain of earthly limitations.

In Heaven, souls feel wonderful emotionally, too. Gone are all of the financial and time constraints, and there are no more pressures or concerns (unless we're inordinately desolate and pull our departed loved ones down emotionally). Someone in Heaven is free to manifest any situation or condition, such as world travel, a beautiful home, volunteer work, and time with family and friends (living and deceased).

I'm frequently asked, "But what if my departed loved ones are mad at me?" People worry that crossed-over friends and family members are angry with them because they:

- Weren't there for them toward the end, or at their last dying breath
- Were involved in decisions to stop artificial life-support systems
- Participate in lifestyle choices that they believe their deceased loved ones wouldn't approve of
- Fought with family members over inheritance issues
- Could have "prevented" their loved ones' deaths or were somehow to blame
- Haven't yet found, or brought to justice, whoever is seemingly responsible for a murder or accident

- Had an argument with their loved ones shortly before they passed on

The fact is, though, that during all of my thousands of readings, I've never met a deceased person who was angry about any of the above matters. In Heaven, you release a lot of the concerns that weigh you down on Earth. You have better clarity about people's true motivations, so your crossed-over loved ones have a deeper understanding of why you acted (or still do act) in certain ways. Instead of judging you, they view you with compassion. They only interfere with your behavior (such as addictions) if they see that your lifestyle is killing you or preventing you from fulfilling your life's purpose.

And don't worry that Grandpa is watching when you shower or make love. These souls aren't voyeurs. In fact, there's some evidence that spirit guides don't see our physical selves on Earth; they perceive our energy and light bodies instead. So they simply understand our true thoughts and feelings during each circumstance.

Since spirit guides are aware of how you actually feel and think, there's no need to hide your worries from them.

Let's say that you have conflicted feelings over your father's death. You're angry because Dad's incessant smoking and drinking contributed to his too-early demise. But you feel guilty, because you believe it's "wrong" to be angry at a dead person, especially your father. Your dad knows just how you feel, because he's able to read your mind and heart from his vantage point in Heaven.

Your deceased loved ones ask you to come clean with them—to have a heart-to-heart discussion about your unresolved anger, fear, guilt, and worry. You can have this conversation by writing a letter to the person who's passed away, by thinking the thoughts you want to convey, or by speaking aloud.

You can communicate with your deceased friends and relatives anytime and anywhere. Their souls aren't located at the cemetery; they're free to travel throughout the universe. And don't worry that you're disturbing their peace. Everyone wants to heal unfinished business in relationships, whether they're living or not, so your departed loved ones are just as eager and motivated when it comes to this discussion as you are.

I find that most people can feel the presence of departed loved ones. Every human body is sensitive to energies and intuitively translates these energies into meaningful knowledge. This is an innate survival skill that you—and every person—possess.

So if you sense the presence of Grandma Betty, *trust this feeling!* Your body knows its surroundings, and it delivers this information to your mind. If you accept your intuitive instincts, you're well on your way to clearly communicating with all of Heaven.

Departed Pets

Your deceased pet can also function as a spirit guide, so far as you may feel, sense, or see its spiritual presence. The soul of the animal lives on, and stays with you as if your mutual love is a leash connecting you both.

When I give workshops, I tell audience members about the dogs and cats I see running and playing throughout the room. Usually we can figure out pretty quickly which dog belongs to which person, because these creatures stay by their owners' sides. These reunions, in which audience members discover that Rover is still around, are quite touching and emotional.

People discover that their pets have the same personalities, appearance, and behaviors as they did while living. If an animal was hyperactive, friendly, well groomed, or amazingly calm, she or he maintains this characteristic after physical death. Playful pups jump in piles of etheric leaves and chase after balls. Whether these leaves, balls, and other playthings are conjured by the dogs' imagination, I don't know.

Cats stay with their owners, too, although they usually don't stick as closely to a human's side as a dog does, due to their independence. So at my workshops, it's difficult for me to tell which felines belong to which people. I have to rely on describing the various cats running around the room, and having their owners "claim" them.

Many of my audience members report that they've seen or felt apparitions of their deceased pets. For instance, you may feel Fluffy the cat jump on your bed, or sense Red the dog lying on the couch. With your peripheral vision, you might even see your pet dart across the room. This is because the corner of your eye is more sensitive to light and movement than the front, so you often see psychic visions out of this area. When you turn to view the image from the front, though, it seems to disappear.

I've seen a few horses and even one guinea pig hanging around like guardian angels. These pets were beloved by their owners, and they continue to stand loyally next to "their people." The animals help by infusing us with their Divine energy of love, and also providing companionship that only our unconscious may be aware of.

I've also noticed spirit totem animals. These are eagles, wolves, and bears who circle their humans' heads, giving them protection and natural wisdom.

I've observed dolphins with people who are involved in oceanography concerns, as well as unicorns around those who are highly creative and sensitive. I've never seen a pet goldfish hanging around, but then again, goldfish go through a very different sort of tunnel of light at the end of their lives, don't they?!

You can maintain communication with all of your deceased loved ones, including your pets, through the processes described in this chapter.

Conducting Mediumship for Others

I've taught mediumship classes since the late 1990s, and during that time I've learned that everyone is capable of communicating with another person's departed loved ones. In other words, we're all equally gifted mediums.

The apparent differences with respect to mediumship skills come down to confidence in trusting one's intuitive feelings and thoughts, as I emphasized earlier. When you're giving a reading to another (especially one who's grief stricken), it's normal to experience some performance anxiety. You naturally feel concerned about giving the person the best possible reading. Well, these anxieties can lessen your mediumship's efficacy.

That's why it's important to focus solely upon connecting with the love between the person in Heaven and the person for whom you're reading. Imagine a stream of nurturing light coming from your heart, as well as the hearts of the other people involved in your reading. Visualize these love lights all merging and blending.

It's important in any reading, but probably the most in mediumship, to put your whole focus upon asking and answering the question "How may I serve?" The ego kicks in with its self-centered concerns such as *What if I get something wrong in the reading?* and *What if I make a fool of myself?*

When you put your entire intention upon helping, in contrast, you automatically conduct the reading from your higher self. And your higher self is 100 percent psychic, 100 percent of the time. Egos, on the other hand, are entirely fear based and therefore not psychic at all. So keep your focus upon service while conducting mediumship for others, and you'll do great!

The departed people with whom you'll connect during mediumship sessions are just people, like you and me. Their only difference is that they don't have physical bodies. Otherwise, they're humans with real feelings and egos. Sure, they may be a bit more

tolerant and forgiving after they get to Heaven, but they still appreciate (and even require) our good manners during mediumship sessions.

For example, departed people know the true nature of your reasons for giving mediumship sessions. They absolutely know whether you're in it because you genuinely care and want to help others, or whether you're mostly interested in boosting your fame and fortune by becoming a famous psychic. Which intention do you think the spirit world is most likely to support?

Departed people appreciate the same social manners as living ones. For instance, please introduce yourself to the person with whom you're trying to connect instead of leaping into demands that they give you information.

- **Do:** "Hi, Claudia. I'm Mary, and I'd love to talk with you to help your grieving niece, Brenda. Would that be okay?"

- **Don't:** "Claudia, give me information for Brenda, now!"

Which salutation would *you* be most inclined to respond to? By the way, you can talk with departed people silently (in your mind) or aloud. They hear you either way, and make no mistake: they pick up on what you're really thinking and feeling, not just what you say out loud.

If your intention is to help, and you mind your manners, the spirit world will cooperate beautifully during your mediumship sessions. Those on the Other Side will give you detailed and accurate messages, which will help everyone involved in the reading.

The spirit world knows that we're wary of ghosts and spooky stuff. So sometimes mediums begin a session with the best intentions, but then when they realize that they're actually talking to a dead person, they get frightened, pull back, and stop the connection.

The spirit world calls this process "hit-and-run readings," and they consider it the height of rudeness. It's the equivalent of starting a conversation with a new acquaintance and then leaving midsentence. Once you begin a reading, stick with it until completion.

The Three Parts of a Mediumship Session

So, how do you know if a reading is complete? Well, this checklist of the three parts of a mediumship session can help. It's also a useful tool for overcoming doubts concerning the reading's validity.

You see, when connecting with someone's departed loved one, the medium typically remains skeptical about the process. Even while he or she is giving a brilliantly accurate reading, the medium's ego usually has a low-level running internal monologue of *I'm just making this up*.

If you're conducting mediumship sessions publicly—on the radio, on television, or in a workshop—then the surrounding audience also maintains some skepticism about their validity. Even the clients for whom you're reading may remain unconvinced, as much as they desperately wish to connect with their Heavenly friends and relatives.

Each time you contact someone's departed loved one, hold this three-part checklist in mind:

1. **Identify the relationship of the departed loved one to your client.** In other words, who is the Heavenly person you're talking to? Is it your client's grandmother, and if so, is it his maternal or paternal one?

2. **Give specific information that elicits a physical response from your client.** You want your clients to be so stunned by the specifics that their heads jolt, their jaws drop, or they gasp or even cry tears of happiness. Strong client reactions help everyone involved in the reading believe in its validity.

3. **Deliver words of love.** This can be a "Grandma's so proud of you" or "I'm truly sorry for how I treated you when I was living" type of message. Any emotional outpouring that touches your client's heart would qualify.

All three parts of the mediumship session are equally important and necessary. It doesn't matter which order you deliver them, as long as you give your client all three.

Here are ways to hit upon these three parts. . . .

The Power of the Name

Your first name carries the vibrational key that unlocks your soul's Akashic records, or your Book of Life. In fact, it's hand-selected by Heaven prior to your incarnation so that it best suits your life's purpose. You or the angels whispered your intended name to your parents before your birth. If they were listening, they gave it to you. If they called you something different, then you'll go through your life feeling like you have the wrong name. Don't worry, though—you can always change it to something that feels more suitable.

Each person's first name has a specific and unique vibration. It doesn't matter how many Johns or Marys there are in the world; each is unique.

So when your clients ask you to connect with their deceased loved ones, you can begin the session by asking, "Is there someone in particular with whom you'd like to connect?" If so, you can ask for the first name of that person.

Then, briefly meditate upon that name and tell your client about the thoughts, feelings, and visions that come to you. Through the power of the name, you'll easily be able to connect with any departed person or animal.

If a person has reincarnated or ascended high above contact level, you'll still be able to discern information about that individual through his or her first name. If he or she isn't personally available, somebody else in the spirit world will be able to deliver messages about the one whom your client wants to contact.

If a person has changed or shortened his or her name (including using a middle, instead of a first, name), then try all the possibilities until you start to get psychic impressions. It's just as if I handed you a key ring that had several keys on it and asked you to open a door for me: you'd try each until one worked. It's the same with people who have shortened or changed their names. Try all the variations until you find the one that results in a flow of thoughts, visions, words, and feelings.

Tell your client everything that you see, hear, feel, and think during the session, no matter how much the ego tries to dissuade you from relaying these psychic impressions to your client. (*Don't say it—it will be wrong!* is an example of the ego's monologue during a mediumship session.)

In fact, the moment you begin a mediumship session, then *everything* that you physically or psychically see, think, and hear is part of it. I mean, everything—without exception. So that ant that walks across the desk during your session is telling you that you're speaking with your client's aunt. The housekeeper who interrupts the session is a sign that one of your client's departed loved ones was involved in cleaning. The airplane that flies over-

head means that your client was in the Air Force, worked in the flight industry, or traveled extensively.

Your gut feelings will supplement and explain the physical signs you'll receive during your mediumship session. The main point is to tell your client everything that comes to you. In fact, I've found that the more bizarre the thought or vision, the more likely that it's an accurate message.

Getting Specifics and Messages of Love

In order to receive the specific details and loving messages that are integral to mediumship, you'll need to have conversations with your client's departed loved ones. Talk to the Heavenly people in the same way that you'd talk with living people. Be real and authentic. Be courteous. Ask lots of sincere questions, and relay the answers you receive to your client, without delay or hesitation.

When your client poses a question for a departed loved one, simply think the question with the goal of asking it of the intended Heavenly person. Then notice and articulate all thoughts, feelings, words, and visions (physical or mental).

When giving an angel reading, you'll get lots of high-level, beautiful sweeping messages. Talking to departed people is a bit different, in that their communications may make no sense to you. That's because the messages aren't intended for *you,* but for your client. The ego may try to convince you to only relay the information you understand, out of fear of getting a wrong answer. Nevertheless, your role and obligation as a medium is to pass along all messages you receive, even if you don't understand them or fear they may be incorrect.

Identifying Who's Who with Your Client

You can discern the identity of the departed loved ones who are with your client by using the chart on the facing page. This is the method that the spirit world taught to me as I went through an apprenticeship of sorts doing thousands of mediumship readings over the years.

At least one departed loved one, functioning as a spirit guide, is with every person at all times. Some people have a huge departed group with them, like a constant spiritual family reunion. The area of the body where each departed loved one appears is based upon "polarity."

Polarity in this chart is based upon a right-handed person. You'd use the reverse for a left-handed person. (By the way, if you were born left-handed and switched to being right-handed, you're still left-handed from an energy standpoint.)

The hand that is dominant (meaning the one you favor) signifies the male side of your body. Imagine a line drawn right down your center, just like in the chart. Everything on the right half of a right-handed person's body has a male energy, and the left has a female energy. So departed people from your father's side of your family stand behind your male side. Your maternal relatives stand behind your female side. In plain terms, if you're right-handed, your mom's relatives are on your left, and your dad's are on your right.

Departed people appear behind your clients, while living ones whom they're thinking about a lot can appear in front. So if you're doing a reading on a client who is worried about her living daughter, for example, you may pick up on the presence of the young female in front of your client's body. Her daughter is definitely alive; she's just on your client's mind enough that she appears in the aura. It's important to know this when doing a reading so that you don't accidentally scare your client into

Positioning of Deceased Loved Ones Around a Person

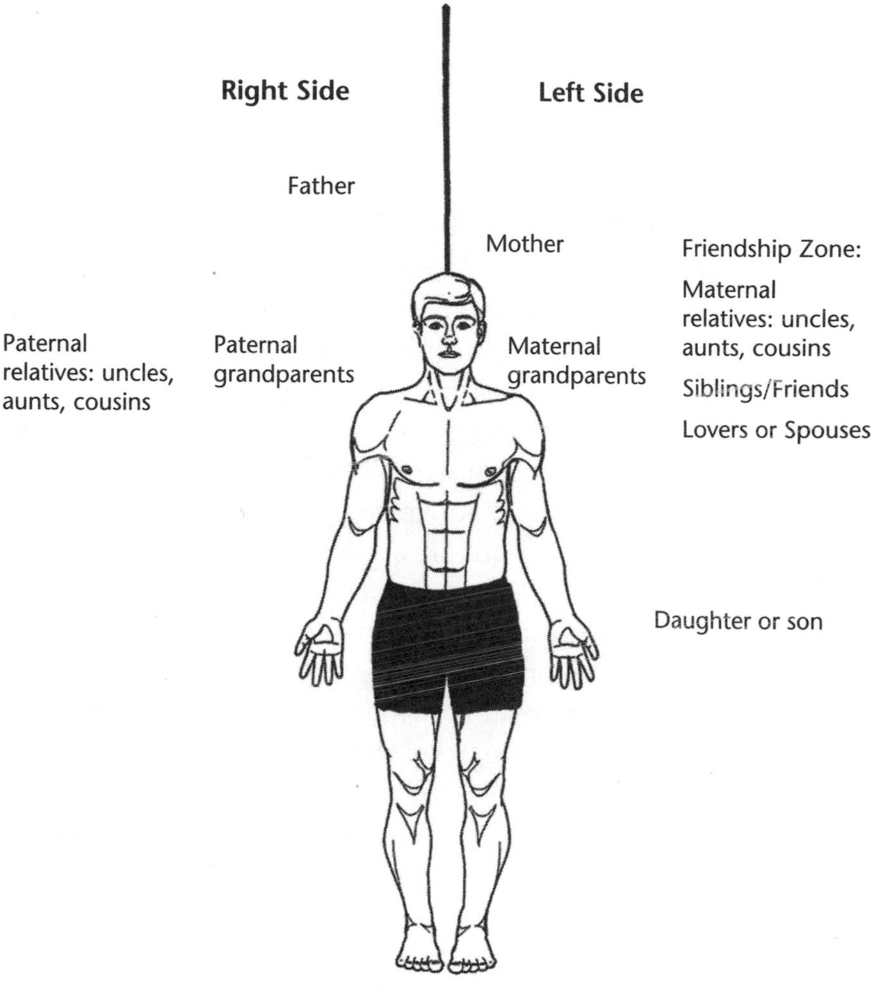

This chart shows the locations and identities of departed loved ones around a right-handed client. Reverse the information for a left-handed client. [Copyright © by Doreen Virtue.]

thinking something has happened to her daughter when you mention her.

The closer the departed loved one appears to the head, the closer that person is genetically. This proximity doesn't necessarily imply emotional closeness. So parents, who are the most genetically related to the client, stand right behind the head. A deceased father would be on the right (male) side of a right-handed client's head, and a deceased mother would be on the left (female) side.

The farther you get from your client's head, the less the genetic connection. Above both of your client's shoulders is what I call the "Grandparent Zone," because this is where you'll find maternal (above the "female" shoulder) and paternal (above the "male" shoulder) grandparents and great-grandparents. Don't let it throw you that a female spirit appears on your client's male side. It's not about the spirit's personal gender. Rather, it's about whether that spirit is a maternal or paternal relative.

Departed friends, siblings, offspring, and in-laws all stand on the female side of your client in an area I call the "Friendship Zone." In the chart, you can see that this is the area from the client's head to where his outstretched hand would be.

You can discern the position and identity of a client's departed loved ones by closing your eyes and scanning around the head and shoulders. Or you can extend your hand and run it closely around your client's upper perimeter and feel for areas that seem warm or where your hand is attracted. These feelings indicate the presence of a loved one. Then compare these locations to the chart. Once you identify the relationship of the loved one to your client, you can ask your client for that departed person's first name. Then use the "Power of the Name" technique described earlier to get information and messages for your client.

Overcoming Blocks to Mediumship

The most common block to receiving mediumship messages occurs when your spiritual frequency is far above that of departed friends and family. If you're most comfortable talking with God and the angels, that means it is dialed at such a high level that you won't hear anything vibrating lower (such as departed people).

You can safely lower your frequency by "grounding" yourself. The easiest way to do so is to rub your bare feet or to go barefoot outdoors. Also, remove any high-vibrational crystal jewelry while conducting mediumship, as it will lift your energy.

With practice, you can give readings of different vibrational levels so that you mix in messages from God, Jesus, archangels, and departed loved ones for the same client. This all comes with intention and practice. You can do it if you have the desire!

I'm frequently asked whether a client's tendency toward being an outgoing extrovert or a quiet introvert will affect readings. Similarly, my students ask whether it's more difficult to read a skeptic than a spiritual believer.

In terms of mediumship readings, the departed loved one's personality is the crucial factor in determining the amount of information you'll receive. For example, I've read for skeptical reporters determined to thwart my mediumship efforts in front of the camera. But because their deceased relatives were outgoing and cooperative, the readings went well enough for the reporters to admit their validity during the filming.

It doesn't matter whether your client's deceased loved ones spoke your language while they were living, or whether they spoke at all (in the case of an infant, pet, or mute person who passed over). The spirit world will translate their messages to you so that you can relay them to your client. Occasionally, I'll have departed loved ones give me foreign-language words to say to my clients. I do my best to relay them phonetically, and find that these words always relate to convincing specifics, which help the client accept the reading's validity.

Contrary to Hollywood films about the deceased, the people in the spirit world are some of the nicest you'll ever meet. They look normal and never display grotesque characteristics. They will appear in the way that best helps identify them. So, for example, if your client lost a baby a decade ago, the child will either show up as a ten-year-old or as an infant, depending upon how that person thinks about his or her offspring. Departed people will appear wearing their favorite outfits, and holding items that help to identify them, such as trademark martini glasses, cigars, knitting needles, golf clubs, and so forth.

Conducting mediumship sessions can be enjoyable and therapeutic. It definitely helps us all to lose fears about mortality and reap the benefits of departed people's messages. One message in particular tends to come through in most mediumship sessions, and I've taken it to heart: "Enjoy each moment of your life, as life is a gift, no matter what."

In Part II of this handbook, we'll continue our exploration of the spiritual and psychic healing methods of Angel Therapy.

PART II

Angel Therapy Methods

CHAPTER 4

Talking with Angels

Since you (like everyone) have guardian angels, and because scientific studies show that intuition is an inherent human characteristic, you *can* have clear conversations with your own and other people's angels. The first step is to address any fears so that they don't hinder your Divine connections.

In my experience teaching angel-communication classes worldwide since 1996 to thousands of people of all ages and backgrounds, I've found that being afraid is the main factor that blocks us. Instead of ignoring the fears, though, it's best to acknowledge and confront them. That way, they won't have power over us.

Here are the most common fears (posed in the form of questions) that people face when they decide to speak to their angels. As you read the following information, notice if it triggers any bodily reactions within you, or any recognition of "This sounds like me!" Give any fears you encounter to Heaven by imagining that each one is surrounded by a ball of light, which you pass to the angels who circle you now. Feel the release as you hand over these concerns. (We'll work with other fear-releasing methods later.)

1. **"Is it blasphemous to talk to angels?"** This fear stems from some organized religions' interpretation of spiritual texts. If you truly believe that you should only speak with God, Jesus, or some other spiritual being, then don't violate that belief. To do so would cause unnecessary anxiety, and we certainly don't want to add to that negative emotion.

However, do consider this: The word *angel,* as stated earlier, means "messenger of God." Angels are gifts from above who act like Heavenly postal carriers, bringing messages to and from the Creator and the created. They operate with Divine precision in delivering trustworthy guidance to us. And just like with any gift, the giver (the Creator) wishes us to enjoy and use it. The Bible and other spiritual texts are filled with positive accounts of people talking to angels, and this natural phenomenon carries into the present day.

2. **"What if I don't receive a message?"** The number one reason why people become blocked with respect to angelic communication is that they try too hard to make something happen. Usually, that strain comes from the underlying fear that they won't be able to hear their angels, or that maybe they don't *have* any guardian angels.

When you contact Heaven, your experience will be influenced by your underlying beliefs. Holding fear-based thoughts will block you from clearly hearing your angels. However, maintaining an optimistic outlook will sharply enhance your angelic connections. The bottom line is: Don't push, strain, or try to force anything to happen. Let God and the angels do all the work of sending you Divine messages. Your job is simply to be receptive and to notice all of the impressions (thoughts, feelings, visions, or words) that come to you.

3. **"What if I'm wrong or just making it up?"** True Divine guidance is uplifting, inspiring, motivational, positive, and loving. Angel messages always mention how to improve something: an outlook, one's health, relationships, the environment, the world, and so on. Angels generally repeat the directive through your feelings, thoughts, visions, and hearing until you take the advised action. If you're unsure if a message is real or not, wait a while, as true Divine guidance occurs again and again, while false guidance eventually fades away if ignored.

Watch out for the very common "impostor phenomenon," in which the ego tries to convince you that you're not qualified to talk to angels and that you don't have intuitive or psychic abilities. Know that this message is fear and ego based.

4. **"Isn't it better for me to learn life's lessons on my own?"** Some people feel that they're "cheating" by requesting Divine intervention. They believe that we're supposed to suffer in order to learn and grow, and that we're responsible for getting ourselves in and out of jams. Yet the angels say that while we can grow through suffering, we can do so even faster through peace. And our peacefulness inspires others in ways that suffering cannot.

The angels won't do everything for you, though. They're more like teammates who ask you to pass the ball as you collectively move toward each goal. As you ask them for assistance, the angels will sometimes create a miraculous intervention. But more often they'll help you by delivering Divine guidance so that you can help yourself.

5. **"How can I be certain that I'm really speaking to an angel?"** God and the archangels, ascended masters, and angels all speak with loving and positive words. Their sentence constructions involve *you* and *we,* as would those of anyone who was talking to you (while the ego will put the word *I* at the beginning

of every statement). Your departed loved ones will use phrases, words, and mannerisms that are similar to those they employed when they were living.

If you ever hear negative words from anyone, living or passed, stop talking to that being and immediately pray for the assistance of Archangel Michael. He'll escort lower energies away and protect you from negativity.

Talking with angels is a pleasant, uplifting experience. Whether you hear them, see them, feel their presence, or receive new insights, you'll certainly enjoy connecting with them.

Handling and Healing Ego-Based Fears

Occasionally, you may doubt the validity of your angelic messages. When this occurs, the angels can help buoy your faith in your spiritual-communication abilities. Here are some tried-and-true methods for handling and healing these fears and insecurities:

— **Ask for a sign.** Even though you may be unsure about whether or not you're hearing your angels, rest assured that they hear *you.* So when you doubt yourself, ask your angels to give you a sign verifying the validity of their messages. You can convey this request mentally, verbally, or by writing it in a letter. Don't tell the angels how you want your sign to appear—just ask them to give you a clear one that you can easily recognize, to assure you that you've correctly heard their messages.

Then, be extra alert for unusual happenings related to the topic of your angelic communications. For instance, if you asked about a particular person, you may hear songs that you associate with that individual, or you might meet people with the same name.

Generally, if you hear, see, think, or feel a message three times or more, it's a sign.

— **Ask for help.** Conversational skills are no different with angels than with living people, in that you must make your needs clearly known. For example, if someone were to talk to you in an inaudible whisper, you'd ask that person to speak up. Or if someone wasn't making sense or was using cryptic language, you'd ask for a clarification of his or her meaning. Don't be afraid to do the same with your angels.

If you can't hear the angels, request that they speak louder. If you don't understand their messages, ask them for additional details.

— **Make sure you really want to communicate.** If you're afraid to communicate with an angel or deceased loved one, then you won't allow it to happen. And Heaven doesn't want to frighten you by forcing messages upon you. Have an honest talk with yourself and your angels to make sure that you truly wish to see and hear them.

— **Turn it over.** Don't carry your doubts single-handedly! Instead, give them to your angels. To do so, you can inhale deeply, and imagine blowing your fears to your guardian angels on the exhale. Or, envision handing over a bubble of fear. They'll take your worries to the Divine light for transmutation, and leave only the lessons and the love. You can also write a letter to your guardian angels about any concerns and ask for their assistance.

Remember: it's not whether you have fears, but how you handle them that counts.

— **Call upon Jophiel.** As explained in Chapter 2, this archangel's name means "beauty of God." One of her roles is to beautify your thoughts so that they're steered away from worry and pessimism, and toward faith and optimism. When you notice your thoughts spiraling into "Ain't it awful" patterns, call upon Jophiel to boost your point of view. Simply think, *Jophiel, please* *help!* and she'll immediately come to your assistance. Please note, however, that if you work with Jophiel, she'll also urge you to beautify your living and work spaces as well. So don't be surprised if you suddenly become motivated to organize your closets!

— **Easy does it.** Be sure that your shoulders are relaxed and that you're breathing deeply while contacting your angels. A relaxed mind and body are the gateway to your psychic higher self. Straining, pushing, or trying too hard to hear the angels puts you into the "unpsychic" lower self of the ego.

If you get uptight during an angel reading, take a moment to center yourself: Close your eyes, let go of time worries, and take three very deep breaths. Picture a beam of white light coming through the top of your head and into your body, magnetizing any stressful energy. Mentally call upon your angels to assist you, and then begin or resume your angel reading.

— **Check your lifestyle.** One reason why angels commonly urge us to improve our food choices, sleep patterns, and exercise habits is because lifestyle affects psychic and intuitive awareness. A heavy chemical-laden diet, along with poor sleep and inadequate physical-fitness routines, clouds thinking abilities and lowers energy levels. Eat, sleep, and exercise for optimal mental alertness, and you'll find that your angelic transmissions greatly improve. Typically, this means adopting a predominantly vegetarian, gluten-free diet, drinking lots of water, avoiding chemicals, setting aside sufficient sleeping time, and working out regularly. Your angels will give you details about the best lifestyle for you if you ask for their guidance. And when angels ask you to change the way you're living, their repetitive advice is difficult to ignore!

— **Practice, practice, practice.** Ultimately, as with any skill, practice helps you develop confidence in your abilities to com-

municate with Heaven, so don't get discouraged if your first few attempts don't yield immediate success. Instead, take an adventurous attitude toward working in harmonious partnership with your angels.

Keep notes in a journal related to your angel-communication sessions. You'll soon notice the accuracy with which your angels predict your future, and guide you in making life-affirming choices. You'll also notice important patterns among your angel messages, which can be a form of Divine guidance in themselves.

CHAPTER 5

The Four "Clairs"

Because you have guardian angels with you continuously, you receive angelic messages every moment of every day. The question isn't *whether* your angels talk to you, but whether you *notice* their communications. That's because angels may speak to you in ways that differ from your expectations.

Angels, along with other Heavenly beings, communicate in four ways:

1. **Through visions:** This applies to things that you see mentally or with your physical eyes; what you see in dreams; signs that appear before you; seeing flashing or sparkling lights; sensing light orbs in photographs; seeing moving objects; or noticing number sequences repeatedly such as 444 or 111. This is called *clairvoyance,* which means "clear seeing."

2. **Through feelings:** These are emotions that come out of the blue, such as joy, excitement, and compassion; physical sensations disconnected to the physical world, such as feeling suddenly warm or feeling changes in air temperature or air pressure; sensing a spiritual presence; feeling as if someone has touched you; or smelling an essence with no physical origin, such as flowers or smoke. This is called *clairsentience,* which means "clear feeling."

3. **Through thoughts:** This is when you know something without knowing *how* you know. It can also mean receiving an "Aha!" revelation; being able to fix an item without instructions; having very wise words come through your speech or writings, as if someone else gave them to you; getting a great idea for a new invention, business, or product; and experiencing "I knew that!" thoughts after something occurs. This is called *claircognizance,* which means "clear thinking."

4. **Through sounds:** This refers to hearing your name called as you awaken; celestial-sounding music from out of nowhere; a warning from a disembodied voice; a conversation or radio/TV program that gives you the exact information you need; a loving message in your mind or outside one ear; or a high-pitched ringing sound. This is called *clairaudience,* which means "clear hearing."

What's Your "Primary Clair"?

While the angels talk to us in a combination of the four ways—visions, feelings, thoughts, and sounds—one of these channels is strongest for you. We call this your "primary clair." The other three clairs amplify and augment this primary means of angelic communication.

You've probably heard that some people are highly visual, while others are more auditory or kinesthetic, and so on. This individual style reflects how you take in the material world with your physical senses, as well as how you receive and notice Divine communication.

To discover your primary clair, think about the following scenarios and then answer the question (choose only one response for each):

1. When you initially meet someone new, what's the first thing you tend to notice about the person?

a. The way the person looks, such as clothing, hair, smile, shoes, or general attractiveness

b. How you feel around the person, such as being comfortable, amused, safe, and so on

c. Whether you find the person interesting, or believe this may be someone who can help you out in your career

d. The sound of the person's voice or laughter

2. Think back on a vacation you took. What stands out most in your memory?

a. The beautiful sights of nature, the architecture, or something that you witnessed

b. The peaceful, romantic, restful, or exhilarating feelings associated with the trip

c. The important and interesting cultural and/or historical information that you learned while traveling

d. The sweet silence, the crashing surf, the chirping birds, the rustling leaves, music, or some other sound

3. Recall a movie that you truly enjoyed. When you think of that film, what comes to mind first?

a. The attractive actors and actresses, the lighting, the costumes, or the scenery

b. The way the movie made you laugh, cry, or moved you in some other regard

c. The interesting plot, or the life lessons that you or the movie's characters learned during the story

d. The musical score or the sound of the actors' and actresses' voices

Note your answers to the above questions. Most likely, you've answered two or three questions with the same letter, which signifies your primary clair, or the dominant way in which you process information about the physical and spiritual world.

This is what the answers mean:

Mostly "a" answers signify clairvoyance. You're a highly visual person and are likely to notice how people, places, and even meals look before you focus on anything else. You're probably very artistic; or if you're not creative in this way, you have an excellent eye for putting together wardrobes, interior design, and such. Visual harmony is important to you, and you appreciate anything that's pleasing to the eye. You probably see sparkling or flashing lights when angels move around you, and you've most likely seen a departed loved one out of the corner of your eye before. You have visions of possibilities, and you have the ability to put these intentions into action.

Your angels speak to you through mental images; signs that you witness with your physical eyes (anything that's meaningful that you see); repeating number sequences (such as 111, 444, and so on); found coins; the sight of butterflies, birds, and colors around people; and other visual means. Trust these visions—they're Heaven's way of speaking to you!

Mostly "b" answers signify clairsentience. You interact with the world through your physical and emotional feelings. You're highly sensitive and may have difficulty dealing with crowds, which can include driving on busy streets and freeways. You sometimes confuse others' feelings for your own. You're very compassionate, and often feel the pain of those around you (sometimes unknowingly). You may overeat or indulge in other addictions to deal with overwhelming feelings. You want to help others to feel happy, and may become a professional helper or form relationships with people who need assistance. You've been teased for being "too sensitive," yet your sensitivity has made you a delicate receiving instrument for Heaven's messages.

Your angels speak to you through your heart and body. You feel joy as an indicator that you're on the right path; dread as a sign that changes and healing are necessary; and fatigue as a clue that you need to take time for rest, play, and self-care. You can tell whether a person is trustworthy or not, and your gut feelings are accurate. You feel air-pressure and temperature changes when communicating with the spirit world, can sense the presence of angels or departed loved ones, and sometimes feel angels brushing your skin or hair. Don't write these sensations off as being "just feelings"—they're how Heaven speaks to you!

Mostly "c" answers signify claircognizance. You're an intellectual who receives direct communication through ideas and revelations. You often know facts (both trivial and important) without having read or heard anything about a particular subject before, as if God has downloaded the information directly into your brain. You're not comfortable with small talk, and prefer deeper and more profound discussions. You may feel uneasy around people, except in one-on-one situations involving a subject of interest to you. You're able to fix electronic and mechanical items without referring to instruction booklets, and you know how to heal people and situations, too. You've most likely been teased for being a "know-it-all." You may be skeptical about angels and psychic abilities, unless you've had a dramatic lifesaving experience that you can't explain away.

Your angels speak to you through wordless impressions that you receive in your mind. You're able to mentally ask for information or help and receive it as Divine instructions that suddenly appear in your thoughts. You receive brilliant ideas for inventions, teachings, and businesses that shouldn't be ignored. The "Aha" moments are clues to when you're connecting with your angels. As a claircognizant, you tend to assume that your knowledge is

common information. It isn't—it's Heaven's way of answering your prayers and speaking to you!

Mostly "d" answers signify clairaudience. You're very sensitive to noise, and you're the first one to cringe at off-key notes or other unpleasant sounds. You can remember song melodies in much the same way that someone with a photographic memory can recall material they've read. It's best if you use earplugs when traveling, as sensitivity to noise makes it difficult for you to sleep or relax on airplanes and in hotel rooms. For the same reason, you avoid the first few rows at loud concerts. When you use alarm clocks, you prefer waking to soft music on the radio rather than loud buzzing sounds.

Your angels speak to you with words that you hear inside or outside your mind. During emergencies, a loud voice outside of one ear warns you of danger. The voice of Heaven, unlike an auditory hallucination, is always loving, to the point, and inspiring—even when it asks you to do something heroic, or function beyond what you believe are your capacities. You're likely to hear celestial music and your name being called in the morning. Don't worry that you're making it up, even if it sounds like your own voice. As long as the voice is loving and asks you to improve a situation, it's Heaven's way of speaking directly to you!

Clearing Your Clairs

Surveys that I've conducted throughout the world have shown that most people receive angel messages through their feelings. The second-most-common way to communicate with angels is through visions. Fewer people tend to get angel messages primarily through their thoughts or by actually hearing words.

You *can* open your primary clair, as well as the other three, to a greater degree. Some methods for doing so include stating

affirmations such as: "I am profoundly clairvoyant," "I easily hear accurate and specific messages from the spirit world," "I clearly understand my angels' messages," and so forth. Avoid using negative affirmations—for example, "I'm just not visual," or "I never receive any messages"—as these can prevent you from further opening your psychic senses. The rule of thumb is to affirm what you desire, instead of what you fear.

Another way to open your clairs is through *chakra clearing.* This involves sending Divine light to the energy centers (called *chakras,* which means "wheels" in the ancient Eastern language known as Sanskrit) in your body that regulate your psychic abilities. The chakras that correlate to each of the clairs are:

- **Clairvoyance:** Third-eye chakra (slightly above the area between the two physical eyes)
- **Clairsentience:** Heart chakra (in the chest)
- **Claircognizance:** Crown chakra (at the top of the head)
- **Clairaudience:** Ear chakras (above each eyebrow)

For a full explanation of chakras and ways to clear and balance them, please see my book *Chakra Clearing* (available from Hay House in hardcover with an accompanying CD).

In addition, the time-tested spiritual practice of working with crystals opens the chakras. Wear or hold the following crystals to heighten each of the clairs (the crystals can be used alone or in combination with each other):

- **Clairvoyance:** Amethyst, clear quartz, moonstone
- **Clairsentience:** Pink tourmaline, rose quartz, smithsonite

- **Claircognizance:** Sugilite
- **Clairaudience:** Phantom quartz, garnet

In the chapters to follow, we'll explore each clair so that you'll recognize the angelic messages that come to you for yourself and your clients. We'll begin by exploring the world of clairvoyance—which means "clear seeing" or the ability to see the energy of the angels.

CHAPTER 6

Clairvoyance, or Clear Seeing

The angels wish to connect with us visually as much as—or even more than—we wish to connect with them. They help us communicate with them by making their presence clearly known. My books *Angel Visions* and *Angel Visions II* (both published by Hay House) contain dozens of stories about people who've had sightings of angels.

What It's Like to See Angels

Many of my psychic-development students mistakenly believe that clairvoyance means seeing angels as distinct, opaque figures who look as solidly three-dimensional as living humans. They expect their visions to be outside of the head, instead of in the mind's eye.

Yet most examples of clairvoyance are similar to the mental pictures you see when you're daydreaming or having a nocturnal dream. Just because the image is in your mind's eye doesn't make the vision less real or valid. When I explain this to my students, they often exclaim, "Oh, so I *am* seeing angels after all!"

With clear intention and practice, most people can develop the ability to see angels outside their mental sphere with their eyes open. In other words, they're able to look at a person and see an angel clearly hovering over his or her shoulders. However, novice clairvoyants usually must close their physical eyes while "scanning" someone. Then they mentally see images of that individual's guardian angels.

Some people see lights or colors in the initial stages of their clairvoyance. Others observe fleeting visions of an angel's head or wings. Some people see angels as translucent and colorless or opalescent, with shimmering hues radiating from them. Still others see them as full-fledged beings, complete with brightly colored hair and clothing.

During stressful times or following intense prayer, some people will have a vivid angel encounter, similar to an apparition experience. While fully awake with their eyes wide open, the person sees an angel, who may look like a human being or take on a traditional angelic appearance, with a gown and wings. The angel is clearly there. The person may even touch or hear the being and not realize that it's a nonhuman until after it disappears.

Photography Orbs

One of the newest ways in which angels are showing themselves to us is by appearing in photographs as orbs of light. If you wish to see evidence of angelic beings, now you can! Their

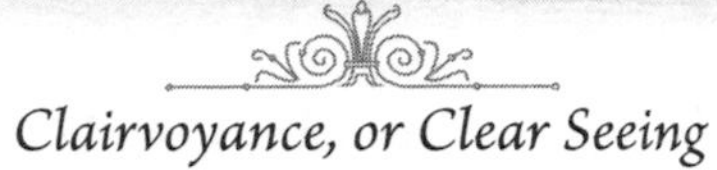

images appear as globes of white light when the pictures are developed. Fairies often appear in photos taken outdoors, and their images look like rainbow-colored orbs bouncing around fields and forests.

The best way to photograph these orbs is by taking a snapshot of a newborn baby or a spiritually minded person. Or try taking pictures when you're at a metaphysically related workshop, especially when the topic is angels. You'll find dozens of these orbs once the photos are developed. This method works best when you hold the intention of seeing the angels while you're taking the photos.

Just as with any other requests for your angels, mentally ask them to appear on film as you snap the pictures. Digital cameras are especially successful at capturing angel images.

Other Angel Visions

Other ways in which we see the angels include:

— **Dreams.** Dr. Ian Stevenson of the University of Virginia catalogued thousands of cases of "dream visitations" in which people interacted with their departed loved ones or angels while asleep. Dr. Stevenson said that the "degree of vividness" is the characteristic that distinguishes mere dreams from true visitations.[1] Visitations include rich colors, intense emotions, and a more-than-real feeling. When you wake up from one, the experience stays with you longer than an ordinary dream. You may remember explicit details about it many years after it occurs.

— **Angel lights.** Seeing sparkles or flashes of light indicates that angels are nearby. You're witnessing the energy sparks as the angels move across your field of vision. This effect is similar to seeing sparks from the back of a car. It's simply friction, and

it means that your spiritual sight is adjusted to viewing energy waves.

The colored lights emanate from archangels and ascended masters (the Appendix lists the various archangels and their associated aura colors). White lights are the glowing evidence of the presence of angels.

About half of my audience members around the world report seeing these sparkles and light flashes on a regular basis. Many people are reluctant to publicly admit this fact for fear that they're hallucinating. They're not. Seeing angel lights is a very real—and normal—experience.

— **Colored mists.** Seeing a green, purple, or other-colored mist is a sign that you're in the presence of angels and archangels.

— **Angel clouds.** Looking up at the sky and noticing a cloud in the shape of an angel is another way that the Divine beings let you know that they're with you.

— **Seeing signs.** Finding a feather, a coin, a stopped clock, or moved objects in your home; seeing lights flickering; or noticing other visual oddities lets you know that an angel is saying, "Hello, I'm here" to you. Departed loved ones often make their presence known by sending birds, butterflies, moths, or specific flowers to you.

— **Having a vision.** Seeing a mental movie that provides you with true information about a person or situation, or that gives you guidance about your life purpose or making changes, is a sign of being in the presence of angels. So is glimpsing a brief image of something symbolic.

For example, when I meet a health-care worker, I invariably "see" a nurse's cap over that person's head. The angels often send this information to us—especially when we're striving to make the world a better place.

Seven Steps to Opening Your Third Eye

An energy center between our two physical eyes, known as the *third-eye chakra,* regulates the amount and intensity of our clairvoyance. Opening the third eye is an essential component of seeing across the veil into the spirit world.

Here are the seven steps to opening your third-eye chakra:

1. First affirm to yourself, "It is safe for me to see." Say this affirmation repeatedly, and if you sense any tension or fear while doing so, breathe deeply. With each exhalation, imagine blowing out your concerns about being clairvoyant (more information on releasing fears follows this section).

2. Take a clear quartz crystal and hold it in your dominant hand (the one that you favor when writing). Imagine a beam of white light coming from above and going into your crystal. Hold the intention that this white light now clear your crystal of any negativity it may have absorbed.

3. Raise the crystal, still in your dominant hand, until it's just slightly above the space in between your two eyebrows. Move your middle finger so that it's pointing through the crystal toward your third eye.

4. Then place the middle finger of your nondominant hand (the one you normally don't write with) at the highest point on the *back* (not the top) of your head.

5. Imagine a powerful and bright lightning bolt coming from your dominant hand's middle finger, going through your third

eye, and then ending up at your nondominant hand's middle finger. You're making a battery circuit, with your dominant hand sending energy and your nondominant one receiving it. As the power runs through your head, it's clearing away psychic debris and awakening your third eye. This process normally takes one to two minutes; and you may feel some pressure in your head, warmth in your fingers, and tingling in your hands. Those are normal sensations from the energy work involved.

6. Next, put your right hand above your right ear, still holding the crystal in your dominant hand. Do the same thing with your left hand and left ear. Imagine white light coming out of your dominant hand's middle finger. Slowly move both hands simultaneously toward the highest part of the back of your head. Keep repeating this motion seven times in a sweeping gesture. Hold the intention of hooking the back of your third eye (which looks just like the back of a physical eye) to the occipital lobe in your head. This is the area of the brain that registers awareness and recognition of your visions. It looks like a thin, round skullcap that you're wearing angled on the back of your head.

With the white light, you're excavating a huge five-inch chamber extending from the back of your third eye all the way to your occipital lobe. This chamber connects the flow of sight from your third eye to the visual part of your brain. In this way, you'll be more aware of the visions that you have, and you'll also understand their meaning.

I've worked with many people who had clean, open third eyes, yet they complained of having no, or limited, clairvoyance. *Having a clean, open third eye is not enough to ensure clairvoyance!* Without the connection between the third eye and the occipital lobe, a person wouldn't be aware of, or understand, his or her visions. It's like showing a movie without having the projector light on.

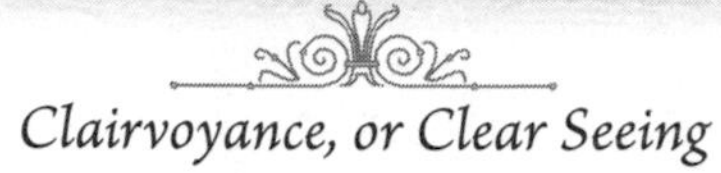

7. The final step is to put the middle finger of your dominant hand on top of the crystal, over your third eye (again, slightly above the area between your two physical eyes). You're going to lift any shields that you may have put over your third eye. With feathery, upward-stroking movements, coax the shield to rise, as if you're opening a window blind. Be sure to breathe while you're performing this step, as holding your breath will slow the process. Repeat the shield lifting at least seven times, or until you sense that each one is lifted.

You can perform this process on another person. If you know an individual who's spiritual and open-minded, especially someone who has experience performing energy healings, have him or her conduct this process on you. While these seven steps can be self-administered, their power is amplified when another person with clear intention (meaning, with a minimum of skepticism) is involved.

After you (or another person) go through these seven steps, you should notice a marked improvement in your mental visions. When you close your eyes and imagine a garden, you'll probably see stronger and more vivid colors and pictures than you did before the process. Your nighttime dreams may become more intense and memorable, and your photographic memory will most likely increase.

Again, the images you see may not appear as something outside of yourself. The mental movies may play on a screen that's inside your head. With practice, you'll be able to project and view those images outwardly. However, whether the visions are in your mind's eye or external is irrelevant. I find that my psychic accuracy is identical whether it's a mental image or something that I see outside of my head. The location of the vision isn't important. What matters is that you notice and give attention to the images, because they're so often visual messages from your angels.

Healing the Fear Blocks to Clairvoyance

If, after going through the seven-step procedure, you still find that your mental pictures are less than you desire in terms of depth, clarity, or color, then you probably have some fears blocking you. These fears are entirely normal, and they can be easily cured whenever you're ready.

For instance, you may be afraid of:

1. Losing Control

The fear: You worry that if you open your clairvoyance, you'll be overwhelmed with visions of angels and dead people everywhere you go. You might also fear that God will try to control you or make unacceptable plans for you.

The truth: Clairvoyance is like a television set that you can turn on, switch off, and dim as you wish. And God's will for you is identical to that of your higher self. The Big Plan has lots of happiness and plenitude in store for you—plus, you'll find greater meaning in all areas of your life.

2. Seeing Something Spooky

The fear: You can't stand haunted houses or monster movies, and you don't want to see anything smacking of ghouls or goblins floating around your home.

The truth: If you've been able to watch the movie *The Sixth Sense* with your eyes open, you've seen the worst. The spirit world is beautiful, something that Hollywood hasn't caught on to yet.

3. Being Fooled

The fear: You have the worry "What if it's my imagination and I'm just making it all up?" or worse, "What if I'm contacted by lower-world spirits who are posing as my guardian angels?"

The truth: The reason why studies show that children have the most verifiable psychic experiences is because they don't get hung up on worrying whether or not it's their imagination. Joan of Arc is quoted as saying to her inquisitors, who asked her if she was imagining hearing the voice of God: "How else would God speak to me, if not through my imagination?" In other words, just because it's all in your head doesn't mean it isn't real, valid, or accurate.

Sometimes I'm asked, "Aren't you worried about being fooled by a demon masquerading as an angel?" This question implies that demons shop at costume stores, drape themselves in white feathers, and—boom!—trap us in their claw-tipped clutches. The fact is that there *are* lower-world energies and beings whom I wouldn't invite to my home for dinner, just as there are living people whom I choose not to hang out with. But this is no reason to shield oneself from seeing clairvoyantly.

I mean, if I asked you if you'd rather walk down a dark alley on the wrong side of town at midnight or at high noon, naturally you'd say noon, right? And the reason? So that you can *see* who's there, of course! Well, the same holds true for the spirit world. Since those unsavory beings are around anyway, wouldn't you rather be able to glimpse who the players are so that you can call upon Archangel Michael to act as a "bouncer" at your home's front door, ensuring that no one gets through without proper ID—assuring that your "guests" are beings of high integrity and a bright inner light?

The inner light is the best indicator of the integrity of a being, whether a living person or someone in the spirit world. With

clairsentience, you can sense a person's character; with claircognizance, you just know that someone is of high integrity or not; and with clairvoyance, you can literally see the glowing light within.

So-called fallen beings in the spirit world can't mimic the huge glowing light that emanates from the belly and radiates upward and outward. These beings could put on an Archangel Michael costume, but they'd lack the essential element: the bright aura that results from living a life of Divine love. In this respect, clairvoyance helps us screen our friends in the physical *and* nonphysical worlds and actually keeps us safe from harm.

You can also *feel* whether you can trust someone or not, whether that being is in the physical or spirit world. You always know—deep down—whether someone is treating you lovingly or not. Trust that feeling in *all* of your relationships! It will never let you down.

4. Being Punished for Something That May Be "Evil" or "Wrong"

The fear: You worry that clairvoyance is the devil's work and that God will punish you for sinning.

The truth: This fear is often based on Old Testament quotes warning about wizards, mediums, and speaking with the dead. Yet in the New Testament, we find Jesus and many others talking with the deceased—and to angels as well. Saint Paul, in his letters to the Corinthians, exclaimed that we all have the gift of prophecy and that we should aspire to these spiritual gifts . . . as long as they're used with love.

And that's the distinction, isn't it? The *Manual for Teachers,* volume III of *A Course in Miracles,* says that psychic abilities can be used in service of the ego (which it says is the only devil in this world) or of the Holy Spirit. In other words, we can harness clairvoyance for love or for fear. If you apply this tool in the service of God and for healing purposes, there's nothing to fear. You'll find that other people's judgments simply roll off of you.

5. Being Ridiculed

The fear: You're afraid of being dubbed "crazy," "weird," "a know-it-all," or "too sensitive" . . . or dealing with the judgmental attitudes of fundamentalist relatives.

The truth: You're probably a "lightworker" or an "Indigo child"—that is, someone who feels compelled to make the world a better place from a spiritual perspective. Lightworkers—and their younger counterparts, the Indigo children—very often feel that they're different or that they don't belong. When people tease you about your spiritual interests or gifts, it compounds that feeling even more. If you were teased during childhood, you may have unhealed emotional wounds associated with various types of ridicule. Ask your angels to intervene, and follow their guidance if they suggest that you seek professional help.

6. Taking Inventory of Your Current Life

The fear: You're afraid of being unprepared to make changes if you see something you don't like about your life—that is, you want to remain in denial.

The truth: Clairvoyance may increase your awareness of parts of your life that aren't working. It's true that taking an inventory may increase your dissatisfaction in certain ways; however, assessing your relationships, career, health, or some other life area doesn't require you to make an immediate 180-degree turn and fix everything at once. Dissatisfaction is a powerful motivator

toward taking steps to improve things. It inspires you to take up jogging, eat more healthfully, see a marriage counselor, and/or devise other methods for healing your life.

7. Seeing the Future

The fear: You may be wary of foreseeing planetary or social changes that are frightening.

The truth: If you "see" these events, and you're absolutely certain that they aren't coming from your ego, then you'll have a better picture of your lightworker mission. You'll be specifically guided as to how you can help the planet avoid, or cope with, these changes. For instance, you may be called upon to pray for peace, send out healing energy, anchor the Light in various places, teach other lightworkers, or heal those who are affected by the changes.

While such an assignment may seem daunting and intimidating, remember that you signed up for it prior to your incarnation . . . and God and the angels wouldn't have given you such a monumental task unless they knew that you could do it. They also provide you with full support along the way—as long as you ask for it and are open to receiving that help.

8. Taking On Too Much Responsibility

The fear: Foreseeing a negative situation, you wonder, *Am I supposed to intervene?*

The truth: Earth Angels are usually just asked to pray about a situation unless it's a very special assignment, and if you *are* supposed to intervene or warn someone, you'll be given very clear instructions about what to do.

9. Not Being Able to Do It

The fear: You worry that you're an impostor who's unqualified to be psychic or to perform spiritual healing. You wonder whether you really have any angels, and if you do, whether you'll be able to make contact with them.

The truth: Everyone feels like an impostor from time to time. Psychologists actually call this fear the "impostor syndrome." Research shows that some of the most competent, successful people are prone to experiencing this condition. It doesn't mean that you *are* an impostor; it just means that you're comparing your insides (which feel anxious in new situations) to everyone else's outsides (which appear to be calm, cool, and collected).

The ego, or lower self, uses sleight-of-hand fears such as this one to distract us from remembering who we are and from working on our life purpose.

Past-Life Blocks to Clairvoyance

Sometimes the block to clairvoyance is rooted in our distant past. Even people who don't believe in reincarnation will agree that significant events in history are still affecting our world today. One is the Inquisition, in which thousands of people were burned, hanged, tortured, and robbed during the 15th century because they had spiritual beliefs or practices that were contrary to the reigning church. The pain of that event, and other "witch hunts" throughout history, still reverberates in the present day as ancient echoes that cry: "Conform to accepted beliefs or suffer the consequences!" Fear is the result, as well as "staying in the spiritual closet"—which leads us to keep our psychic abilities and spiritual beliefs a secret.

But how do you know if a past-life wound is blocking your clairvoyance? The signs include the following:

- You consider yourself to be non–visually oriented—that is, you don't visualize easily, you rarely remember dreams, and you don't really focus on how people or things look.
- You've had few, if any, psychic visions.
- You feel tense or worried every time you think about opening up your clairvoyance.
- You have an undefined sense of anxiety about becoming psychic, as though you'd get into trouble or be punished by some individual or even by God.
- When you think about people being burned at the stake or hanged, your body reacts strongly with chills, shivers, breathing changes, or tension.

In contrast, here are the signs that childhood experiences have blocked your clairvoyance:

- You saw angels, sparkling lights, or deceased people when you were a child, but your psychic visions diminished as you grew older.
- You're a highly sensitive person.
- You were teased for being "crazy," "evil," or "weird" as a child or adolescent.
- You worry what your family would think if you revealed your psychic gifts.

- You're afraid that if you opened up psychically, you'd make life changes that would disappoint or harm your loved ones.

A past-life regression by a certified hypnotherapist, or via a vehicle such as my audio program produced by Hay House called *Past-Life Regression with the Angels,* is the most effective way to release these blocks. Your unconscious mind won't frighten you with memories that you can't handle, so please don't worry that a regression will overwhelm you.

Trying Too Hard

By far the most common block to clairvoyance is trying too hard to see. As I touched upon earlier, when we push or strain to do anything, we get blocked. That's because any type of pressure stems from fear, which originates in the ego—and the ego is 100 percent *not* psychic.

We try too hard when we fear, deep down, that we might not be able to achieve something and attempt to force it to happen. The underlying negativity, however, can undo hours of positive affirmations and manifestation efforts. The fear becomes a negative prayer that, unfortunately, attracts self-fulfilling prophecies.

Healing Psychic Blocks

Everyone has psychic blocks to one degree or another, so the point isn't to be completely clear of them . . . the objective is to be *aware* of them and deal with them promptly as they arise. Sometimes we become ashamed of our blocks, and we don't admit them to ourselves or others. Yet blocks are nothing to be ashamed of. They are, however, areas of our lives that require our attention.

"Healed healers" (to borrow the term from *A Course in Miracles*) aren't people who are without issues—that would nearly be impossible in this world. Rather, they are those who are *aware* of their issues and strive to avoid letting them interfere with their Divine life mission.

Nonetheless, we can mend and release hang-ups that block us psychically. These healing techniques and tools can also have markedly positive results on other life areas, in addition to clairvoyance:

— **Healing during sleep.** When you're sleeping, your skeptical mind is also at rest. That's why it's a perfect time to engage in spiritual healing. With the skeptical mind asleep, your ego can't block the angels from performing miraculous clearings on you. So, as soon as you're ready to open up your clairvoyance, ask your angels and anyone else in the spirit world with whom you work to come into your dreams. An example of how to do so is to pray:

"Archangel Raphael, I ask that you enter into my dreams tonight. Please send healing energy to my third eye, and wash away any fears that could be blocking my clairvoyance. Please help me see clearly with my spiritual sight."

— **Cutting cords to family members.** If you realize that you're afraid of your mom's judgments about psychic abilities, for instance, you can use the cord-cutting techniques described in Chapter 12 and direct them specifically toward cutting the cords of fear connected with your mother. Repeat the process for any person (family member or otherwise) whom you worry would have a negative reaction to your clairvoyance. In addition, cut the cords with any individual from your past who ridiculed or punished you for being psychic.

— **Support from like-minded souls.** When I was preparing to "come out of the spiritual closet" and admit my clairvoyance publicly, I was naturally concerned about negative consequences. I was fortunate enough to become acquainted with a university-trained internal-medicine doctor and psychiatrist in private practice in Newport Beach, California, who was also acknowledging for the first time that he was a clairvoyant. A recent head injury during an accident had opened up his third eye, and he found that he was able to see inside his patients' bodies. He could also see the chakra systems and the negative emotions trapped inside of them, but he was afraid of openly admitting his clairvoyance, thereby risking his medical license and reputation.

We motivated, supported, and counseled each other with respect to going public about our clairvoyant gifts. We kept reminding one another that if we weren't true to ourselves, we really couldn't help our clients in the best possible way.

I think *you* will also find it helpful to have the encouragement of someone else who's in a similar situation. Pray for such a person to come into your life, and you'll be guided to him or her. You can also consciously look for support at metaphysical meetings held at bookstores, New Thought churches such as Unity or Religious Science, psychic-development courses, or Internet bulletin boards related to the intuitive arts.

— **A past-life-regression session or CD.** About half of the psychic blocks that I see in my audience members stem from their past-life wounds related to being psychic. As I mentioned earlier, it makes sense to go through a past-life regression to clear them. Most certified hypnotherapists are trained in giving such regressions. Your only task is to find one with whom you feel comfortable, because your trust in the regressionist is key to your ability to let go and allow your unconscious memories to surface.

Alternatively, you can use a taped past-life regression such as my *Past-Life Regression with the Angels* CD.

— **Positive affirmations.** I'm amazed by how many bright, knowledgeable metaphysicians complain to me that they're "just not visual." When I point out that this statement is a negative affirmation, they realize that these words are blocking their clairvoyance. Then they begin using positive statements to describe what they desire, instead of what they fear.

"I am highly visual" and "I am profoundly clairvoyant" are examples of positive affirmations to say to yourself, even if you don't yet believe that they're true. Trust me—reality always catches up to your affirmed thoughts!

— **Calling on the angels of clairvoyance.** There are specialist angels for every situation, and psychic development is no exception. The "angels of clairvoyance" monitor and minister to your third-eye chakra, helping you develop spiritual sight. Mentally say:

"Angels of clairvoyance, I call upon you now. Please surround my third eye with your healing and clearing energy. I ask for your help in fully opening my window of clairvoyance now. Thank you."

You'll probably feel tingles and air-pressure changes in your head—especially between your two physical eyes—as the angels of clairvoyance do their healing work.

— **Lifestyle improvements.** There's a huge correlation between how well you treat your body and the vividness of your clairvoyance. Your visions are always sharper, more detailed, and more accurate when you're engaged in a consistently healthful lifestyle. Exercise, proper rest, getting outside regularly, eating a

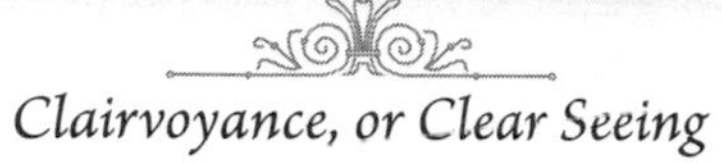

light plant-based diet, and avoiding toxins in food and beverages help you to be a clearer channel of Divine communication.

After using one or more of the preceding healing processes, your clairvoyance should be noticeably brighter and clearer.

Visions from Heaven

Your angelic experiences may involve what you see, either while awake, asleep, or meditating. There are many ways to sort the true visions from the false ones.

A True Angelic Experience Involving Seeing

- Dream visitations almost seem surreal, with vivid colors and emotions.

- You see sparkles or flashes of light or colored mists.

- There's a feeling of spontaneity and naturalness to the vision.

- You experience repetitive instances of seeing a feather, coin, bird, butterfly, rainbow, number sequence, and so on, beyond chance occurrences.

- You receive service-oriented visions of yourself helping others.

Imagination or False Guidance Involving Seeing

- Dreams seem ordinary and forgettable.
- You see worst-case scenarios without being given instructions on how to avoid them.
- You get the feeling that you're forcing the vision to occur.
- You look for a sign but find inconsistency or force the meaning that you want onto what you see.
- You receive an ego-centered vision of yourself gaining at the expense of others.

Next, we'll look at clairsentience, which is the most common way we receive messages from angels.

CHAPTER 7

Clairsentience, or Clear Feeling

An emotional or physical feeling is the way in which most people experience their angels. When angels come extra close, you can "feel" their presence. Many people I interview can recall when they sensed a specific spirit nearby. Most say something such as "Yes, I could feel my mother with me the other night. It seemed so real, but I still wonder if I was just imagining it."

You may tend to discount your intuition and not trust yourself. How many times have you had a gut feeling to *not* get involved in a certain relationship, take a job, buy something, or drive a particular route? How often did you then override your feelings, do it anyway, and later regret it?

Of course, whether or not you listened to your inner guidance, such situations give you opportunities to learn to have faith and follow your higher self the next time. This is the process for

communing with your angels—that is, it has to do with trusting that your feelings are a legitimate and accurate divining device, which God installed in you.

Common Ways in Which You Feel a Spiritual Presence

Here are some of the common ways you may connect with your angels through your feelings:

- Catching a whiff of flowers when there's no blossom nearby
- Feeling that someone has touched you, stroked your hair, nudged you, protected you, tucked you in, or hugged you
- Noticing an air-pressure change, a sense of tightness around your head, a feeling that something is pounding on your forehead, an impression of some spiritual essence moving through your head, or a sensation similar to being pulled underwater

You may also experience:

- Air-temperature changes
- A sudden surge of euphoria or bliss
- A gut feeling that this experience is surreal (even if you're reluctant to share it with others)

True angelic experiences are warm, safe, loving, and comfortable; while false ones make you feel cold, prickly, and afraid.

You can also use your feelings to "test-drive" an intuitive sensation and notice how you react. For instance, let's say that you're getting an urge to move to a new area. You're conflicted, however, wondering how such a change would affect your family, friends, and career. Even though some of these factors aren't clear to you, you can "try on" your future and get a better grip on your Divine guidance.

As you imagine what it would be like to stay living where you are, focus on your feelings. Is your heart full of relief, sadness, joy, or some other emotion? Does any part of your body tighten or relax in response to the mental image?

Now, compare your emotional and physical sensations when you imagine what it would be like to move. Your feelings are very accurate gauges of your soul's desires and your Divine will, which is one with God's will.

How to Increase Your Clairsentience

If you normally don't have a strong sense of your emotional or physical feelings, you can use the following methods to open this important channel of Heavenly communication. When you become more sensitive to your emotions and physical sensations, life becomes richer and relationships deepen . . . and you feel greater compassion and Divine love, understand others more readily, become more balanced, and are more apt to notice and follow your intuition.

Here are some steps that can increase your clairsentience:

— **Sleep next to clear quartz crystals.** You can purchase a clear quartz crystal "point" (a cylinder with a point at the end) fairly inexpensively at any metaphysical bookstore or gem show. Place the crystal in sunlight for at least four hours to clear away any psychic residue from its previous owner. Then, put one or more of these crystals on your nightstand or beneath your bed. If they're on the nightstand, position them on their sides, with the points facing your head. If the crystals are below your bed, have the point facing up, toward your head or your heart.

As you become more sensitive, you'll probably have to move the crystals so that their points face away from you. You may even need to reposition them farther from your bed. Highly sensitive clairsentients sometimes develop insomnia when crystals are too close to their sleeping area.

— **Work with the aroma of pink roses or rose essential oil.** The aroma of pink roses opens the heart chakra, which is the energy center that regulates clairsentience. Keep a pink rose nearby and breathe in its fragrance often, or purchase some high-quality essential oil made with real—not synthetic—rose. Put the oil over your heart, and dab some near your nose so that you can frequently enjoy its aroma.

— **Wear a rose quartz necklace.** Just as pink roses open the heart chakra, so does rose quartz crystal. This beautiful pink stone is attuned to this energy center. In addition to activating your clairsentience, rose quartz crystals can help you open up to romantic blessings in your life.

— **Increase your sensitivity to physical-touch exercises.** Close your eyes and handle an object on your desk. Touch it slowly and deliberately, noticing the minute details and textures. Rub the item along the back of your hand and your arm, and be aware of the sensations. Have a trusted friend gently blindfold you and hand you unknown items to touch or food samples to taste. Put all of your awareness on your physical and emotional sensations, and try to guess what each thing is.

— **Tune up your body with cardiovascular exercise and light eating.** When you feel tired, heavy, or sluggish, it's more difficult to discern your feelings. Jogging, brisk walking, yoga, or other cardiovascular exercise helps you more precisely pinpoint the meaning and messages behind your clairsentience. Similarly, eating light, healthful foods keeps you from being weighed down. A sense of heaviness or being stuffed with food can block your awareness of Divine guidance. Anything that can make your body feel better—including massage, a nap, or a bubble bath—will heighten your sensitivity to your gut feelings.

Protecting Yourself

Clairsentients often complain that they're *too* sensitive. "I absorb the toxic energy of other people's problems," and "I get overwhelmed because I can feel everyone else's emotions," are the two chief complaints among the feeling-oriented set.

Ironically, clairsentients often enter professions that increase their likelihood of physical contact with others. Massage, energy healing, medicine, and counseling are a few common occupations among people who understand the world through their feelings. And while feeling-oriented individuals are excellent at those professions, they must take measures to ensure that they don't absorb residue from their clients' negative emotions.

There are two ways to deal with this issue: preventive measures and clearing activities. Preventive measures involve shielding yourself from others' toxic energies. Clearing activities entail releasing any such energies that you *do* absorb, including those that stem from your own fearful thoughts.

Shielding

Preventive measures are a little like birth control—they're not 100 percent effective, but they do provide considerable protection.

There are dozens of ways to shield yourself, and I'm just including my two favorites. . . .

1. **Music.** The angels say that music acts as a psychic screen, surrounding us with protective energy. In stressful situations, then, it's a good idea to have it continually playing around us.

Music is not only a preventive measure; it's also a clearing measure. Archangel Sandalphon is the angel of music, and he works with Archangel Michael to clear away the effects of negativity. Call upon Sandalphon to help you select the best music for various situations. Have a CD playing when you meditate, and ask Sandalphon to work with the melody to shield and clear you.

2. **Pink light.** The angels taught me this method one day when I was at the gym. I said hello to a woman I'd never met before whose path crossed mine on the free-weights floor. She began telling me about her numerous medical operations in minute detail. I knew that she needed to express herself and wanted a friendly ear. However, I was also aware that she was spewing out toxic energy with her endless discourse on illness and disease.

I mentally called upon my angels for help. *"Surround yourself with a tube of pink light,"* they immediately counseled me. I envisioned myself encircled by a tall cylinder of pink illumination, as if I were inside a lipstick tube. It extended above my head and below my feet.

"You've never liked shielding yourself with white light," the angels reminded me, *"because you felt as if you were cutting yourself off from others. Since your life's mission specifically calls for you to interact with people and not isolate yourself (as you did in your most recent past life), you have shied away from using the white-light shield."*

Their words were true. Although I knew all about shielding methods, I rarely used them because I wanted to be there for my clients. I'd once worked with a psychiatrist who counseled people from behind a gigantic oak desk. I'd always thought that he used it as a buffer to avoid emotional intimacy with his patients—it was also a power symbol. I didn't want to employ white light during my counseling sessions, because it felt like I was isolating myself from my clients.

The angels continued: *"But notice how this pink shield of light is very different. See how it radiates intense Divine love energy out toward this woman. Notice, also, how it projects beautifully strong Heavenly energy inward toward yourself. And nothing can permeate this pink-light shield but energies that originate from Divine love. So, in this way, you can be fully present for this woman, without taking her illusions of suffering upon yourself."*

Since that day, I've been using the pink-shield technique with great results—and positive feedback from those I've taught it to. Thank you, angels!

Clearing

We sometimes feel tired, irritable, or depressed without knowing why. Often the culprit stems from our contact with other people's negative mind-sets. If you work in a helping profession, your exposure to toxic emotions is especially high, and it's essential to clear these energies from yourself regularly.

You can clear yourself with etheric cord cutting and vacuuming (both are described in Chapter 12). Still, the simplest way to rid yourself of psychic debris is with the help of Mother Nature. Just as plants convert carbon dioxide into fresh oxygen, they also transmute lower energies. Greenery is especially helpful in ridding your body of energetic toxins.

The angels urge us all to keep a plant next to our bed—a potted one on the nightstand can do wonders while we sleep! It absorbs the heavy energy that we've ingested during the day and sends it into the ethers. Don't worry . . . it won't harm the plant.

If you work with people in any way, but especially as a massage therapist or counselor (where you're open to receiving your clients' released negativity), place plants near your workstation. You'll feel more refreshed at the end of the day by taking this one simple step! The angels say that broad-leafed plants work best because the wide surface area absorbs greater energy fields. So a pothos or philodendron would be a good choice. Avoid prickly or pointy leaves in the plants that surround you. Interestingly, feng shui, the ancient Chinese art of spatial arrangement, also recommends staying away from pointy-leafed varieties. Apparently, their swordlike leaves don't promote positive energy flow.

Being in Touch with Your Feelings

With practice, you become increasingly tuned in to your feelings and are more apt to trust their wisdom.

A True Angelic Experience Involving Feelings

Such an encounter may:

- Feel warm and cuddly, like a loving hug
- Make you feel safe, even if it's warning you of danger
- Often be accompanied by unexplained fragrances of flowers
- Leave an indent in the couch or bed, as if someone has just sat next to you
- Cause air-pressure or temperature changes

- Feel like someone is touching your head, hair, or shoulder
- Cause you to be sleepy or hyper afterward
- Give you a deep belief that "this is real"
- Create repetitive and consistent gut feelings to make a certain life change, or to take a certain step
- Feel natural, as if the experience is coming to you freely

Imagination or False Guidance Involving Feelings

Such an experience may:

- Feel cold and prickly
- Make you afraid and panicky
- Have no sense of smell associated with it, or an unfamiliar and unpleasant odor
- Feel like someone is sexually fondling you
- Cause the room to feel ice-cold
- Give you a sense of being all alone
- Be followed quickly by a return of normal feelings
- Result in a deep belief that the experience wasn't real
- Cause gut feelings that urge you to change your life, but with different themes and ideas that come from desperation, not from Divine guidance

- Have no sense of familiarity to it
- Feel forced, as if you're willing the experience or guidance to happen

If you add to your spiritual repertoire with the power of your thoughts and ideas, you'll have another clear avenue to receive and follow your Divine guidance. Next, we'll examine the power of claircognizance, or thoughts from Heaven.

CHAPTER 8

Claircognizance, or Clear Thinking

When there's some tidbit of knowledge that you know for sure, without knowing *how* you know, it's called *claircognizance,* or "clear knowing." Maybe this has happened to you: You're arguing with a person about a topic that you're only vaguely familiar with, but something deep inside of you tells you a fact or two, and you cling to this knowledge without having evidence to support it. Your companion asks, "But *how* do you know?" And you have no retort other than "I just know—that's all."

You've probably been called a "know-it-all" a few times in your life, and this proclamation has a grain of truth to it. You *do* know a lot, but you're totally puzzled about how you came to own all this information.

Many great inventors, scientists, authors, futurists, and leaders have used their gift of claircognizance to tap into the collective unconscious and access new ideas and inspiration. Thomas

Edison, for instance, said, "All progress, all success, springs from thinking." It's said that Edison and other great inventors meditated until they received a brainstorm of inspiration and ideas.

The difference between someone who simply receives such information and a person who also benefits from it is the ability to accept what's happening as being useful and special. So many claircognizants write off their incoming transmissions as information that's glaringly obvious to others. *Everyone knows this stuff,* claircognizants will say to themselves. Then, a couple years later, they find that the brilliant idea they'd conceived has been carried out and marketed by another person. So, the challenge for those who receive their Divine guidance as a thought, idea, or revelation is to accept that this is a unique piece of information that *really could be the answer to their prayer.*

Let's say that you've been praying for Divine guidance to help you leave your job and become self-employed. You then receive an idea for a business that would help others, and this thought comes to you again and again (two characteristics of true Divine guidance). Will you discount it, thinking, *Well, everyone dreams of self-employment, so obviously this is pie-in-the-sky wishful thinking?*

I've found that claircognizants benefit from spending time away from the computer and office by getting a healthy dose of nature and fresh air. Many thinking-oriented people lead work-centered lives, creating a need for balance in the areas of physical fitness, playfulness, family matters, spirituality, and relationships. Even focusing a little extra time on these things can help a claircognizant feel more clear in following ideas that are born of the Infinite Mind.

Judgment vs. Discernment

Those who favor a "thinking" style with regard to angelic communication may have higher intelligence quotients (IQs) than most. After all, they're usually avid readers, with a wide range of interests that would land them higher-than-average IQ scores.

A key ingredient in tapping into that intellectual awareness is being able to differentiate between when you're using discernment versus when you're relying on judgment. There are key differences between these two intellectual behaviors that can determine spiritual outcomes.

Let's start with an example involving cigarette smoking. You're probably aware of the many studies linking this habit to various diseases and health risks. Discernment would say, "I'm not attracted to smoking or smokers. I don't care for the smell of cigarettes or their effects." Judgment would say, "Smoking is bad. Smokers are bad." Notice the difference? One operates under the Law of Attraction, which simply asks you to honor your personal preferences without labeling or condemnation.

In a similar vein, when you're unsure whether or not an idea is Divinely guided, pay attention to your internal mechanisms of discernment. The old adage "If in doubt, don't" has a lot of wisdom to it. Your inner computer knows if something is off or not. You might not need to reject an entire idea, but you may have to rethink or revise certain components of it.

You may need to seek out specialists in areas that are outside of your expertise. If this is the case, mentally ask God and your angels to lead you to these individuals, and you'll delight in seeing how quickly they appear.

I experienced this phenomenon when I felt that I was supposed to write a book on vegetarianism. I knew that I needed to find a collaborator who was a registered dietitian with a spiritual bent—one who was also familiar with vegetarianism. With full faith, I turned my request to find such a person over to God. Three weeks later, at one of my workshops, a registered dietitian named Becky Prelitz introduced herself to me. She had come to see me speak because she was very immersed in spiritual teaching

and living. *This is the woman I'm looking for!* I thought. The more I talked to Becky, the more convinced I became that she was the expert who was the answer to my prayer. Today, Becky (and her husband, Chris) is a great friend; and our book, *Eating in the Light: Making the Switch to Vegetarianism on Your Spiritual Path,* was published by Hay House in 2001.

Common Ways in Which Claircognizance Occurs

Here are some of the ways in which you may have already received Divine communication through your thought processes:

- You met a new person and suddenly knew details about him or her without having had previous knowledge of the individual.

- You possessed information about something related to current events without having read or heard about it.

- You had a premonition of how something (a business venture, a recreational trip, or a relationship, for example) was going to turn out . . . and you were right.

- You had an idea for a business, a book, or an invention that haunted you. You executed the idea and found that it worked out favorably. Or, you ignored it and discovered that someone else with the same idea ran with it and made a fortune.

- You lost your checkbook, keys, or wallet; and when you asked your angels where the item was, you received a sudden knowingness that led you right to it.

True Divine claircognizance is repetitive and positive. It speaks of ways in which you can improve your own life and the lives of others. It's service oriented, and while a certain idea may make you rich and famous, that's a side benefit and *not* the motivation behind the concept. In fact, it's usually these types of altruistic ideas that lead to benefits for their inventors. Those who pursue self-serving ventures often repel potential clients and customers, who sense the hollow values behind an idea.

My publisher and mentor, Louise L. Hay, once told me that her financial life finally healed when she began focusing on how she could serve, rather than on what she could get. When I applied this same principle to my own life, I found that it had remarkably curative effects on my level of happiness, as well as on my career and income.

True claircognizance helps you do something that will truly help others, in such a way that it will inspire people to seek you out as customers, clients, sponsors, audience members, publishers, and so forth. This force comes from the Creator, Who knows of your true talents, passions, and interests, and how these characteristics can be used to help others. In biblical times, money was referred to as "talents," and *you* have talents that you can exchange for money.

True claircognizance doesn't just wave a dream under our noses and then taunt us to discover how to manifest it. No! It gives us complete, step-by-step instructions. The trick, though, is to remember that God only teaches us one step at a time. We receive this information in the form of repetitive thoughts (or feelings, visions, or words, depending upon our spiritual orientation) that tell us to *do something*. The "something" usually seems insignificant: call this person, write this letter, attend this meeting, read this book, for example. If we follow the directions and complete Step A, then in the same repetitive manner, we're given

the next set of instructions for Step B. Step-by-step, God guides us all the way to the realization of our intended manifestation.

We always have free will, so we can ignore the guidance anytime we choose. However, most people find that if they don't complete one of the Divinely guided steps, they feel stuck, as if they're spinning their wheels in the mud. I always ask people who tell me that they feel blocked, "What piece of Divine guidance have you been repetitively receiving but are ignoring?" Always, I find that this insight (which they're avoiding because of some fear of making a life change) is the key ingredient they've been searching for.

Angels give you ideas in response to your prayers for guidance. You receive this Divine transmission at moments when your mind is receptive, such as during dreamtime, meditation, exercise, or even while watching a television program or movie (when your mind tends to go on cruise control). You'll feel excited and energized by Divinely guided insights, and it's important not to counteract them with pessimistic thoughts. The idea rings true, and you'll know—deep in your soul—that this is it! Certainly, any idea can fail. *But it can also succeed!* And trying is what gives your life meaning at the end of the day.

If you've had some negative experiences with respect to following hunches in the past, you could understandably feel gun-shy now. You may have decided to play it safe and secure by avoiding major life changes. That's fine, as long as you're happy with your current circumstances! But if there's an area of your life that's off balance, it's natural for you (as well as God and the angels) to want to heal the situation. That's called achieving "homeostasis," which is the instinctive drive to attain balance that's common to all living things.

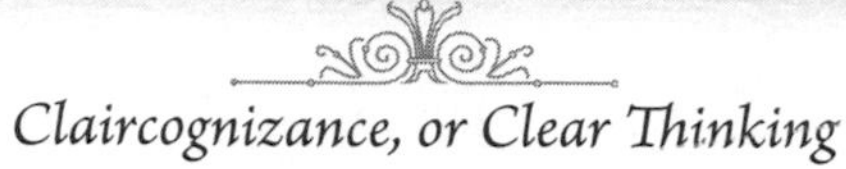

Skepticism, Pragmatism, and Faith

More than those with the other Divine guidance styles, claircognizants tend to waver when it comes to faith. When you're a thinker, it's easy to think yourself into a box of skepticism. Faith seems illogical and rests upon so many intangible factors.

Yet a good scientist always experiments before drawing a conclusion. Whether your hypothesis is geared in favor of believing in angels or not, take the time to put the theory to a test. For instance, God and the angels hear your thoughts (don't worry—they don't judge them), so you can call upon Heaven without eliciting raised eyebrows from your colleagues.

Mentally ask your angels to help you with some area of your personal or professional life. Then, notice what help comes to you after you've made your request. It could be an instant response, where you have a strong impulse or idea, or it may come in a more tangible fashion, where a person will "just happen" to hand you a journal article with the information you seek. The two key ingredients in this experiment are: (1) *asking* for guidance (the Law of Free Will prevents Heaven from helping without our giving permission), and (2) *noticing* the help that's being received.

Being aware of this type of assistance is entirely different from holding a forced scavenger hunt where you're searching for clues. False guidance is always the product of struggle and worry. True Divine inspiration comes easily on natural wings of love.

The more you can learn to trust and follow such information, the more you'll benefit from your internal guidance system. For instance, you may get an idea about opening a new business. The idea is foolproof, and you wonder why you never thought of it before. You venture forward, and all the doors open for you: financing, location, partnerships, and more. The business is a rapid success, and you know that you were guided by true Divine wisdom.

How to Increase Your Claircognizance

Since claircognizance can come about subtly, as a thought or an idea, it's easy to miss this high-level method by which Heaven communicates with us. You might dismiss your Divinely inspired idea without recognizing it as an answer to your prayers. You could mistake it for an idle thought or a daydream, instead of embracing Heaven's inspiration.

Claircognizants also ignore their Divine guidance because they believe that what they know is obvious to others. "Everybody knows that!" claircognizants will decide, and won't capitalize on the brilliant idea that they just received. It doesn't help that many have been teased for being know-it-alls, so they hesitate to speak up for fear of being ridiculed. Yet this label has a kernel of truth to it, for claircognizants are very tapped into the collective unconscious.

So, it's important to really pay attention to what enters your mind . . . that includes the repetitive thoughts and also the novel ideas. Divine guidance comes both as suggestions that hammer away at you repeatedly and also as lightbulb-type inspirations. One of the best ways to pay attention to this form of guidance is to keep a daily journal where you have a conversation with yourself about your thoughts and ideas. The journal format could be like an interview with your higher self, perhaps set up in a question-and-answer format. In this way, you can more easily bring unconscious information to your awareness.

When you get a response, don't second-guess yourself. Instead, give your thoughts and ideas a moment to speak up. Ask them, "What do you want to tell me?" It could be an insight such as "This new person I've just been introduced to doesn't seem honorable." Or it could be an inspired idea that helps you *know* the truth about a spiritual principle, or a walloping brainstorm for a can't-miss new business.

By keeping a journal, you can assess the patterns and accuracy of your thoughts and ideas. You'll get in the habit of gaining awareness about which ones are truly Divinely inspired. You've probably had the experience of ignoring your thoughts and saying later, "I *knew* that was going to happen!" or "I *knew* I shouldn't have gone there!" Your successes and mistakes teach you both to trust and follow your insights.

I also find that many people who are thinking oriented (as opposed to feeling, sight, or hearing oriented) tend to be workaholics. They often hole up in their offices, strapped to the chairs in front of their computers. All this work is fine, as long as it's balanced with time spent outdoors. Yet I usually have to urge claircognizants to go out in nature. It's foreign to their comfort zones! Once outside, though, claircognizants find that the fresh air, plants, and trees help sharpen their psychic senses. They become even more open to, and aware of, their Divine inspiration.

The peace of the outdoors makes it easier to hear our thoughts and take note of clever ideas. As we clear room in our schedule for personal time-outs, we take a break from the world of clocks and telephones. We become more tuned in to the inner rhythm of our bodies—and all of nature. Among other benefits, spending regular time outdoors helps us develop "good timing," which really means that we notice and follow the rhythm of life. When we return to the office, we've developed more acute instincts with respect to the best moment to make that phone call, send that e-mail, or speak up at that meeting. Our time outdoors might also inspire us to break away from the office completely and forge a career that matches our hearts' desires more fully.

Trusting Claircognizance

Some people are skeptical about following their intuition because they've done so in the past and have been burned as a result. Perhaps you had a great idea one time, but when you followed through on it, everything turned into a mess, so you're reluctant to ever trust your ideas again.

Usually, these situations involve two types of patterns:

1. **Our initial idea was Divinely inspired, but then fear took us off the path.** When we initially received the idea, it was based upon true Divine guidance, which always stems from love. But somewhere along the way, we got scared. This fear blocked our receptivity to continued guidance and creative ideas, took us off our original inspired path, and triggered behavior and decisions that originated from the ego. When we partner with our egos, unhappiness and errors inevitably follow.

For instance, a woman I know named Bernice had a wonderful idea to start a home-based business as a personal fitness trainer. The idea seemed perfect, as it was a service that would help others in a field that she enjoyed, and it would allow her to stay home with her toddler while earning some money. So Bernice quit her day job and opened the business at her home. The first month, five people signed up as clients, which provided Bernice with enough income to pay her bills plus have extra money left over.

Yet Bernice worried whether her initial success would continue. *Where will my new clients come from?* she fretted. After ruminating on her future for several days, she decided to purchase advertising in several newspapers. She also bought full-color brochures, with matching stationery and business cards. Her expenses for these investments were high, but Bernice decided that she needed to "spend money to make money."

The next month, Bernice only signed up one new client. She worried even more about her business and spent additional money on advertising. But nothing that she tried seemed to work, and within four months, Bernice decided to return to her previous job to ensure that she'd bring in a steady income.

What happened? she wondered. In reviewing her situation, we find that Bernice truly did receive Divine guidance in starting her business. This was reinforced by her initial success, which gave her enough money to pay her bills, with a surplus afterward. It was only when Bernice began to let fear creep into the picture that things started to dry up. That's also when she started forcing things to happen through misguided advertising and unnecessary purchases. Her expenses went up and her income went down because she began listening to her ego's fears rather than her higher self's reassurance and guidance.

2. **Instead of acknowledging our Divine guidance, we forced something to happen, or we listened to another person's opinion and ignored our inner teacher.** Sometimes we want to hear what we want to hear, so we'll decide that "he's the guy," even if our intuition (and our best friend) is screaming that he's a creep. Or, we'll decide that God wants us to quit our job and move to Sedona, Arizona, when our gut feelings urge us to make a gradual career transition. In some cases, we'll betray our intuition and do something that's against our better judgment simply because a strong-willed person talks us into it.

True and False Claircognizant Guidance

So, how *do* you know if an idea is God-inspired brilliance or a route to a wild-goose chase? With regard to thoughts, ideas, and revelations, the characteristics to notice are:

- **Consistency:** True guidance is repetitive, and the idea will stick with you over time. Although it may build in detail and application, the core notion will stay the same. False guidance changes its course and structure constantly.

- **Motivation:** True guidance is motivated by a desire to improve a situation. False guidance's chief aim is to make you rich and famous. Although true guidance may yield those rewards, they are side benefits and not the central motivation for the idea.

- **Tone:** True guidance is uplifting, motivating, and encouraging. It urges you on, saying, "You can do it!" False guidance is the opposite, shredding your confidence to pieces.

- **Origination:** True guidance appears quickly, like a lightning bolt, in response to prayer or meditation. False guidance comes slowly, in response to worry. When you get an idea, back up and examine the trail of thoughts preceding it. If you were worrying about something, your ego may have conjured up a scheme to rescue you. If you were meditating peacefully, however, your higher self had the room to truly connect with the Divine collective unconscious and has probably handed you a gem of an idea.

- **Familiarity.** An idea that comes from true Divine guidance generally fits in with your natural inclinations, talents, passions, and interests. False guidance usually contains "left field" advice involving activities that hold no interest for you.

By noticing these characteristics, you can increase your faith in the ideas that you follow. You'll know that you're on the right path, and you'll use all of your higher intentions to create success. A healthy confidence level correlates to holding clear, laser-focused thoughts that lead to rapid manifestation.

If you combine your claircognizance with the ability to hear the voice of the Divine, as we'll discuss in the next chapter, you'll take your idea-manufacturing process to an even higher level.

Receiving Heaven's Messages as Thoughts

Your experiences with your angels may involve ideas, revelations, or thoughts rather than your feelings. Many of the world's great thinkers and inventors get their innovative ideas from the ether. Here's how to sort the true from the false:

A True Angelic Experience Involving Thoughts

Such an encounter may:

- Involve concepts that are consistent and repetitive
- Have a central theme of how you can help solve a problem or help others
- Be positive and empowering
- Give you explicit instructions about what step to take right now, and provide instructions for subsequent steps once you complete the first one.
- Bring exciting ideas that energize you

- Come out of the blue or in response to prayer
- Call for you to take human steps and do some work
- Ring true and make sense
- Be consistent with your natural interests, passions, or talents

Imagination or False Guidance Involving Thoughts

Such an experience may:

- Be random and ever changing
- Have a central theme of how you could get rich or famous
- Be discouraging and abusive
- Get you thinking about worst-case scenarios
- Consist of depressing or frightening thoughts
- Result in ideas coming slowly, in response to worry
- Be a get-rich-quick scheme
- Seem hollow and ill conceived
- Be unrelated to anything you've previously done or been interested in
- Have a primary motivation of desire to escape a current situation, rather than helping others

In the next chapter, we'll focus upon hearing angelic messages, which is known as clairaudience or "clear hearing."

CHAPTER 9

Clairaudience, or Clear Hearing

I think it's ironic that I, a former psychotherapist who once worked in locked hospital psychiatric wards, now teach people how to hear voices! Yet, when we listen for the voice of God and the angels, it's the sanest sound we'll ever hear. It can show us love in the face of seeming chaos and provide us with logical solutions when challenges arise.

Hearing the voice of Spirit is called *clairaudience,* or "clear hearing." Let's discuss what it is, and how to increase its volume and clarity.

Common Ways in Which You Hear Heaven's Voice

Chances are excellent that you've heard your angels and other spiritual beings speak to you throughout your life. Have any of the following situations happened to you?

- Upon awakening, you hear your name called by a disembodied voice.
- Out of nowhere, you detect a strain of beautiful, celestial-sounding music.
- You hear a song repeatedly, either in your head or on the radio.
- There's a loud, shrill ringing noise in one ear.
- You overhear a conversation in which a stranger says the exact thing that you need to hear.
- You just "happen" to turn on the television or radio at the precise moment when a relevant discussion is occurring.
- You pick up on a loved one's call for help, and it turns out that he or she needed assistance just then.
- A disembodied voice gives you a warning or a life-enhancing message.
- You're looking for a lost item, you pray for assistance, and then you hear a voice tell you where to locate it.

Answers Come in Response to Questions

God and the angels speak to us in response to our queries, so we can kick-start a conversation simply by directing a question to them.

One time I wanted to know why certain Christian factions promoted the idea that it was beneficial to "fear God." I just couldn't understand why anyone would be afraid of our loving Creator, or why a person would *aspire* to fear Him. So I asked my angels to help me understand this belief system. No sooner had I posed the question than I was scanning the radio stations in my car and the scanner stopped on a Christian talk show. At that very moment, the host began explaining why Christians "should" fear God. I didn't agree with his message, but I was very grateful to receive the answer to my question . . . especially so quickly after asking.

Is there a question that you have or some area of your life in which you desire guidance? Take a moment right now and mentally ask God and the angels about it. Hold the intention of giving that question to Heaven, and trust that you'll receive an answer. Even if you can't hear any Divine beings answering you right now, be assured that they can definitely hear *you!*

You should receive an auditory response to your question within a day or so. Sometimes you'll hear the answer in the form of a song. You may notice a tune playing repeatedly on the radio or in your mind. The answer to your question might be in the lyrics. Or, if the song reminds you of someone, it could be a message that this person is thinking about you.

Usually when we hear a voice call out in the morning, it means that our angels or guides simply want to say hello to us. It's easiest for them to deliver this greeting when we're just waking up because our lucid mind is more open to spiritual communications. We're also more apt to remember the message when half-awake, as opposed to being fully asleep. If they have another revelation to add to their greeting, they'll specify that message to us at the same time. So when you hear your name called, don't worry that someone wants to get through to you. It's simply a loving greeting to let you know that you're being watched over.

If, after asking Heaven a question, you don't receive a reply, it could be that you've overlooked it. Or maybe you don't want to hear the information that Heaven is sending you because you didn't appreciate the guidance you were given at some time in the past. Thus, you block yourself from picking up on any new messages. Keep repeating the question until you obtain the answer. Ask your angels to help you hear, and it will happen eventually.

A spiritual-counseling student of mine named Tienna was frustrated because she'd been in my psychic-development course for three days and still hadn't heard from her angels. Tienna complained that during her angel readings, she only heard staccato—one- or two-word messages. For instance, she was giving a reading to a classmate and heard the words *uncle* and *car accident* in her ear. Well, it turned out that Tienna's classmate had lost an uncle in a car accident.

"But I want to hear more than just one or two words!" Tienna said. "I want to have full-on conversations with God and the angels."

I asked Tienna's angels for help, and I heard them say to her, *"Just stay in the class, Tienna. With persistence and patience, you will hear us soon."* I relayed that message to my student.

By the fifth day of our spiritual-counseling class, Tienna bounded up to me excitedly. "I hear them, I hear them!" she exclaimed. She'd had a clairaudient breakthrough in exactly the way her angels had predicted: through a persistent intention to hear, and through patience in surrendering "when" that would happen. From that day forward, Tienna had full-blown auditory discussions with her angels, who gave her both personal guidance and information for her clients.

Ringing in the Ears

Many lightworkers report hearing a high-pitched ringing sound in one ear. It's a shrill noise that can be painful and intrusive. When checked by a physician, tinnitus (a disturbance of the

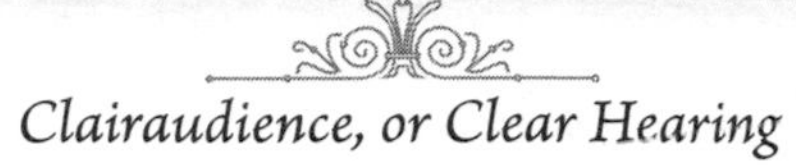

auditory nerve) is usually ruled out. That's because the ringing is of a nonphysical origin. It's a band of woven information, encoded in electrical impulses. Heaven downloads guidance, assistance, and information through this bandwidth, which sounds like a computer modem hooking into the Internet.

Sometimes the ringing is accompanied by a pinching or pulling sensation on the earlobe. This happens when angels and guides especially want your attention. You don't need to consciously understand the message encoded within the ringing sound—you just need to commit to receiving it. The information will be stored in your unconscious, where it will positively influence your actions, ensuring that you don't procrastinate with respect to your lightworker mission.

Please don't worry that the ringing could be coming from a lower or dark source. The sound shows that the energetic frequency of the encoded information originates from a high place of Divine love. Lower forces wouldn't be able to work with such an elevated frequency.

The ringing sound is actually an answer to your prayers for guidance about your life's mission. If it becomes too loud, sharp, or intrusive, mentally tell your angels that it's hurting you, and ask them to turn down the volume. The information will still be transmitted to you; it will just come to you in a quieter fashion. If the earlobe pinching or pulling becomes painful, tell your angels and guides about the discomfort, and ask them to stop.

When I petitioned my angels and guides to turn down the volume of the ringing and to stop hurting me with earlobe pinching, I was never again bothered by loud tones or painful ears. The angels certainly aren't offended by our requests. They need our feedback so that they best know how to help us.

"How Do I Know Who's Talking to Me?"

If you're concerned about the true identity of a voice that's speaking to you, simply ask your "caller" to identify him- or herself. If you don't believe or trust the answer that you receive, ask the spiritual being to prove his or her identity to you. As you'll discover, the entity will say or do something that will stir beautiful emotions within you, or you will be confronted with something that only that particular being could know or accomplish. Here are some guidelines:

- God's voice sounds very loud, to the point, friendly, and casual, with good humor and modern vernacular.
- The archangels are very loud, to the point, formal, and direct. They speak a lot about Divine love; getting on track with your mission; and overcoming doubts, fears, and procrastination with respect to this purpose.
- The angels sound almost Shakespearean at times, with very archaic and formal speech patterns.
- Your higher self sounds like your own voice.
- The ego comes across as abusive, discouraging, paranoid, and depressing; and it begins sentences with the word *I* because it's egocentric.

How to Increase Your Clairaudience

We're all naturally psychic, and this ability includes clairaudience and all of the other "clairs." As I've mentioned before, we usually find, however, that each person possesses one primary channel of Divine communication.

It's similar to a four-cylinder automobile engine: all four cylinders work and are equally important; however, one cylinder fires first, before the others. Your primary clair drives the engine of your Divine guidance.

If you're naturally auditory, you already hear the voice of God and your angels. However, if this isn't your primary channel of Divine communication, you may struggle to pick up on Heaven's voice. You may read about accounts of people who receive warnings or messages from their angels, and wonder, *Why don't my angels talk to me?* Here are several methods that can help you hear the voice of the Divine, loud and clear:

— **Clear the ear chakras.** As we've discussed, each of the psychic senses is governed by a chakra energy center, and clairaudience corresponds to the two ear chakras.

The ear chakras are located above the eyebrows, inside the head. They appear to be a violet-red color. Imagine two violet-red disks spinning clockwise above your eyebrows. See or feel yourself sending them beams of cleansing white light and illuminating them from the inside. Notice how clean and large they become. Repeat this method daily, or whenever you feel that your psychic hearing is clogged.

— **Release psychic debris.** If you've been verbally abused by others or by your own self-deprecating talk, your ear chakras are probably polluted with toxins from the negative words directed toward you. Mentally ask your angels to surround you with comforting energy.

You can release the pent-up negativity in your ear chakras by writing down the names of those who've verbally abused you (including yourself) and putting the paper in a plastic container of water. Then, place it in the freezer compartment of your refrigerator. You'll have an immediate sense of release as you put these names in the freezer. Keep them there for a minimum of three months. (By the way, this is a wonderful method of releasing *any* kind of problem.)

— **Reopen tuned-out frequencies.** As a child, did you tune out the voice of your mom, your dad, your teacher, or some other person—perhaps even yourself? When you were a kid, your ability to shut out incessant nagging or other verbal unpleasantness may have been your only available defense mechanism. The trouble is, though, you may have tuned out *all the other* voices in the frequency range of those you originally blocked. So you may have difficulty hearing a Heavenly voice that's in the same pitch or tone as your mother's, for instance. You might not hear your higher self if you tuned your own voice out long ago.

Fortunately, you can simply "change your mind" to reopen your physical and spiritual ears to the full range of frequencies. Since your firm intention to shut out sound was the origination of the blockage, simply make a different firm intention to now hear all ranges of sound frequencies.

— **Increase your sensitivity to sound.** Take time each day to notice the sounds around you. For instance, tune in to birds singing, children laughing, and cars driving by. Also, notice the sounds that accompany ordinary behaviors, such as turning the pages of a book, writing a note, or breathing. By paying attention to subtle and not-so-subtle sounds in your environment, you heighten your sensitivity to the voices of the angels and your guides.

— **Protect your physical ears.** As your sensitivity to the sound frequency of the angels increases, you'll find that loud noises bother you more than they did before. You'll need to cover your ears when you're in an airplane that's landing and avoid front-row seats at loud rock concerts, for instance. You'll also have to ask friends to speak more quietly to you on the telephone, request restaurant tables that are away from noisy groups of people, and secure hotel rooms positioned far from the elevator and ice machines.

— **Ask your angels.** Some people have quiet angels and introverted spirit guides. Just as you do when you're having a conversation with a living person, don't be afraid to ask whomever you're conversing with: "Would you please speak a little louder?" Our celestial friends really want to communicate with us, and they need our honest feedback to help guide them in knowing the best way to make their voices heard.

My mother, Joan Hannan, was having difficulty hearing her angels and guides, so she asked them to speak louder. But she still couldn't hear them, so Mom said in a powerful voice, "Please, speak even louder!" She then heard her grandmother's voice say very distinctly, "I'm right here!" My great-grandmother seemed to mean, "You don't have to yell—I'm standing right next to you. I can hear you just fine!"

You're always in control of your Divine communication, and if you want Heaven to turn *down* the volume or intensity of your auditory messages, just ask.

Hearing Heaven's Messages

In popular culture, hearing voices is taken to be a sign of insanity. In contrast, many of the world's saints, sages, and great inventors have received guidance in this way. Prior to my carjacking experience, I heard a loud, clear voice warning me. And thousands of people have told me of receiving similar warnings

that saved them or their loved ones from danger in ways that defy normal explanation.

The difference between hearing a true Divine voice, heeding the imagination, and having a hallucination is clear and distinct. I'll give you quite a bit of information about distinguishing between messages from your angels and your imagination. As for hallucinations, several scientists point out key distinctions.

Researcher D. J. West gave this definition of the difference between a hallucination and a true psychic experience:

> Pathological hallucinations tend to keep to certain rather rigid patterns, to occur repeatedly during a manifest illness but not at other times, and to be accompanied by other symptoms and particularly by disturbances of consciousness and loss of awareness of the normal surroundings. The spontaneous psychic [now often called "paranormal"] experience is more often an isolated event disconnected from any illness or known disturbance and definitely not accompanied by any loss of contact with normal surroundings.[1]

Psychiatrist Bruce Greyson, M.D., studied 68 people who were prescreened clinically to rule out schizophrenia. Dr. Greyson found that exactly half of these subjects reported having an apparition experience, where they had seen a deceased loved one with their physical eyes open.[2]

Psychic researchers Karlis Osis, Ph.D., and Erlendur Haraldsson, Ph.D., noted that during most hallucinations, the people believe that they're seeing a living human being. During psychic experiences involving visions, they believe that they're seeing a celestial being, such as an angel, a deceased loved one, or an ascended master.[3]

Heaven may speak to you through a loud, disembodied voice outside your head; a quiet inner voice inside your head; a conversation that you "happen" to overhear; or music in your mind or heard over and over again on the radio.

A True Angelic Experience Involving Hearing

- Sentences usually begin with the words *you* or *we*.
- There's a sense that someone else is talking to you, even if it sounds like your own voice.
- It's readily apparent how the message related to your immediate concerns or questions.
- The voice is to the point and blunt.
- The sound is loving and positive, even if it's warning you of danger.
- The voice asks you to take immediate action, including changing your thoughts or attitude to be more loving.
- The voice calls your name upon awakening.
- You become aware of strains of beautiful, disembodied "celestial" music.
- You receive a message about self-improvement or helping others.

Imagination or False Guidance Involving Hearing

- Sentences usually begin with the word *I*.
- It feels like you're talking to yourself.
- The message is muddy, cryptic, or unclear.
- The voice is wordy and vague.
- The tone is taunting, alarming, or cruel.

- The message involves gossip and speculation about others.
- You hear abusive words.
- You experience loud, unpleasant noises or discordant music.
- There's a message to hurt yourself or others.

Paying Attention to the Messages

Whether your angelic messages come to you as a vision, a voice, an idea, a feeling, or a combination of these four elements, you can distinguish true from false guidance by paying attention to the characteristics. Be assured that if you're facing danger before it's your time to go, your angels will give you very loud and clear guidance, regardless of the form in which it appears.

Everyone has an equal ability to communicate with their angels, because all people are equally "gifted" spiritually. Some may appear to be more psychically adept than others; however, that's only because those individuals have been willing to listen, believe, and trust the input of their spiritual senses.

As I've emphasized, the single biggest block I find in my psychic-development students is that they try too hard to make an angelic experience happen. They want to see and hear an angel so desperately that they strain to do so. But anytime people grasp for something, they're coming from a place of fear. It could be an anxious thought of *Maybe I won't be able to see or hear, Maybe I don't have angels,* or some other vague ego-based concern. The ego isn't psychic at all, being entirely fear based. Only the love-based higher self within each of us is able to communicate with the Divine.

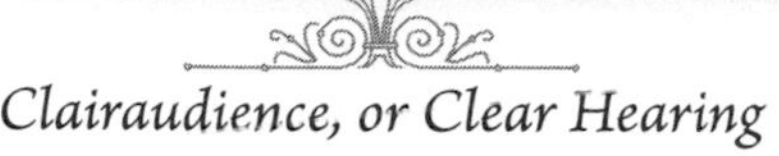

So the more you can relax, the more easily you'll be able to consciously commune with your angels. The breath is a wonderful starting place, as is optimism akin to what many children have. They say, "*Of course* I have angels. Everyone does!" Children don't care whether they're imagining their angelic visions; they simply enjoy and accept them. As a result, kids easily see and hear their guardian angels. If you stopped worrying whether your Divine connection is real or not, you'd overcome the ego's blocks and enjoy your higher self's natural—and very real—gifts.

The angels say:

"Fear is a natural predator of the psychic domain. It robs your psyche of its creative control and asks you to allow it to dominate your moods, schedule, and decisions. It weakens you, who are all-powerful. Your decision-making capability is impaired at its behest. Allow no terror to 'inter-fear' with your domain of happiness, for that is God's kingdom of great blessings. You're more powerful than any anxious force. Your Divine willingness can overcome any darkness that the world has ever seen. Your Creator's light will always blind any enemy if you will but focus on this radiance within your mind."

So, instead of doubting our ability to connect with our angels, let's look at how we already do receive messages from Heaven and how we can enhance that connection even more. Next, we'll learn how to give an angel reading for someone else.

CHAPTER 10

How to Give an Angel Reading

My life purpose isn't to give angel readings and spiritual healings to clients. It's to teach *other people* how to do these things for themselves and *their* clients. I always encourage my spiritual-counseling students to teach others—to create an ever-spreading ripple effect that increases the awareness that we *all* have angels, that we *all* can communicate with them, and that we *all* have spiritual gifts we can use to help ourselves and the world.

The main difference between a psychic and an angel reading is that in the former, psychics normally receive information from spirit guides, while in the latter, the guidance comes from God and the angels. An angel reading involves much more than giving a fortune or telling the future. It means teaching empowering and life-affirming messages and spiritual tools so that clients know how to contact their own angels. It also

usually involves conducting some Angel Therapy healing methods, such as those outlined in Chapter 12.

I want to share the exact steps that I teach my psychic-development students so that you can give yourself and others angel readings.

How to Give an Angel Reading

An angel reading is similar to a psychic one, except that you're directing the questions to guardian angels and spirit guides for the purpose of healing some life area, and/or for guidance about someone's life mission.

It's best to give an angel reading to a person you don't know really well who's open-minded and nonjudgmental. A new friend in a spiritual study group would be an ideal angel-reading partner. Still, you can definitely do a reading for a family member or old friend. It's just that your ego will scream at you: *I already knew that about this person!* If you can ignore the ego's rantings, you can give a reading to anyone, whether you know the person or not.

Let's begin with a mutual angel reading, where you and another person are reading each other simultaneously. Begin by saying a prayer to whomever you're aligned with spiritually:

"Please help me to be a clear channel of Divine communication. Please allow me to clearly hear, see, know, and feel accurate and detailed messages that will bring blessings to my partner and me. Please watch over this reading and help me relax and enjoy it. Thank you, and amen."

Next, sit facing your partner. Then both of you should take a metal object from your body (such as a watch, a ring, a necklace, a belt buckle, a hair clip, glasses, or car keys) and hand it to the other person. Each of you should hold the metal item that you received from your partner in the hand that you normally don't write with. This is the one where you receive energy—your "receptive hand."

Then, hold your partner's free hand with your own. Place your hands where they'll comfortably rest for the next few moments, such as on your or your partner's knees or lap. Now, I'd like to take you both on a vacation, okay? Please close your eyes and breathe in and out very deeply. . . .

> *Imagine that the two of you are in an exquisite purple pyramid that has magically transported you to a white sandy beach in Hawaii. The purple pyramid lands with a gentle plop on the sand and opens up, forming a natural blanket for the two of you. It is a perfect day on the island, and since this is a completely isolated beach that's only accessible by boat or plane, you and your partner have total privacy.*
>
> *You feel the gentle summer breeze blowing across your skin and through your hair. You smell the delicious salt air and hear the waves' melodic crash upon the shore. You feel a beam of sunlight dance warmly over the top of your head, as if it were going right in and illuminating the inside of your mind and body.*
>
> *Off in the distance, you notice a pod of dolphins swimming playfully in the ocean. You tune in to these creatures, and you feel them send you a huge wave of Divine love energy. As your heart swells with warmth and gratitude for these beautiful animals and this perfect day on the beach, you realize that you're* <u>one</u> *with the dolphins. And then this realization extends even further: you are* <u>one</u> *with all of the life in the ocean—including the sea turtles and the colorful tropical fish—and you're also one with the waves, the sand, and the sun.*
>
> *You realize that you're one with all of life, including your partner. And so you mentally affirm to your partner,* <u>You and I</u>

are one . . . you and I are one . . . I am you . . . and you are me . . . you and I are one. You realize that this oneness that you share is real. Although you may look different on the outside, on the inside you and your partner truly do share one spirit, one light, one love. You mentally affirm to your partner: One love . . . one love . . . one love.

As you revel in this knowingness, you also realize that you're one with all of the angels. As you scan your partner with your physical eyes closed and your spiritual sight wide open, imagine what it would be like if you could see your partner's angels in your mind's eye. What might they look like?

Do you see any that look like small cherubs? How about medium-sized angels? Really large ones? You might see these beings in full detail in your mind's eye, or as fleeting glimpses. Or, you might simply feel or know their presence.

As you scan around your partner one more time, notice any other angels that may be present. If one or more of these beings especially attracts your attention, tune in to them now by holding the intention of connecting with them.

Even if you don't see anyone around your partner, or you're unsure of yourself, you can still receive accurate messages from your partner's angels that will bring blessings to him or her. As you breathe in and out deeply, hold the intention of having a silent conversation with these beings.

Then, mentally ask them, What would you like me to know about my partner? Repeat the question as you take note of impressions that come to you in response. Be aware of any thoughts, words, mental pictures, or feelings that arise as you continue to ask the question What would you like me to know about my partner? Don't try to force anything to happen. Simply trust that the answers are coming to you now, and notice even the subtlest little thought, feeling, vision, or word in your mind.

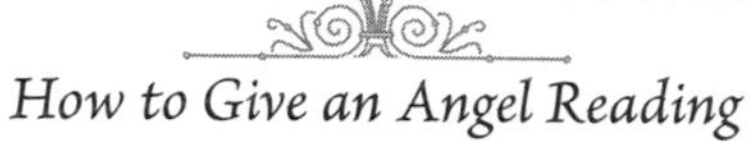

Next, mentally ask your partner's angels, What message would you like me to tell my partner, from you? Again, be cognizant of any impressions that come to you as thoughts, feelings, visions, or words. Don't judge or discount these impressions. Simply view them with detachment.

Then, mentally ask your partner's angels, Is there anything that you'd like to tell me? Be sure to breathe while you take heed of the answer.

Finally, mentally ask these angels, Is there anything else that you'd like me to tell my partner? Again, listen for the response from many levels.

The most important part of giving an angel reading is having the courage to tell your partner everything that you received, even if you're unsure about the information or worry that it may offend the person (you can always pray for a diplomatic and loving way to deliver potentially offensive messages). While the angel messages may make no sense to you, they'll probably make perfect sense to your partner. Spend the next few moments, then, sharing everything that you saw, felt, heard, or thought during your mutual angel reading.

Answering Questions During an Angel Reading

When you give someone an angel reading, you can answer their questions with the angels' guidance. The key is to get out of the way and tell your client everything that you see, hear, think, and feel during the reading (exactly like the mediumship sessions described in Chapter 3).

Relay to the angels any questions that your client poses to you. Feel or see yourself as an intermediary who sends them Heavenward, and then receives the answers through your mind and body.

Your role and obligation is to tell your client everything that you receive, without hesitation. If you're unsure of an answer, you can say so, but still share the information.

Usually, clients understand the answers and you don't. That's because in an angel reading you function like a telephone for Heaven. Phones don't hesitate or argue before delivering a message. They're simply a conduit, just as you are during angel readings.

Here are the most common questions you're likely to receive while conducting an angel reading:

"Do I Have Angels?"

The answer is always a resounding "Yes!" This question comes from those who are new to angels. It's an opportunity for you to pass on the great news that everyone has guardian angels who are nondenominational and unconditionally loving and approving.

"Who Do You See Around Me?"

Your client doesn't actually care if you *see* which angels or guides surround her. The question actually is: "Who do you *discern* around me?"

Some clients are in search of a specific departed loved one, while others pose this question because they're curious about their celestial angels. Sometimes people inquire because they want to know if they have *anyone* with them.

You can answer the question by closing your eyes and mentally scanning your client's head and shoulders. You can also scan with your hands skimming (but not touching) your client's upper perimeter.

Notice any areas that draw your attention. Then breathe and tune in. Focus upon any feelings (emotional or physical), visions (no matter how fleeting or fragmented), thoughts (even if you think they're about yourself), and sounds or words.

Say to the being around your client, "Please tell me about yourself," and then relay the reply to your client.

If your client is seeking a specific departed loved one, then please use the information and chart in Chapter 3, and if they'd like their angels' names, please utilize the method outlined in Chapter 2.

"What Is My Life Purpose?"

This question normally means: "Which job would give me a sense of happiness and meaning, while simultaneously guaranteeing that I could pay my bills?" Occasionally, though, someone will ask it as a way of determining their spiritual path. So, you may need confirm with your client which direction they're inquiring about.

Each person has a personal life purpose, which means something that he or she is here to learn during this lifetime. Examples are patience, forgiveness, compassion, balance, and boundaries.

Some people (called the lightworkers) also have global purposes in addition to their personal ones. A global purpose is some contribution that your soul elected to make during your lifetime. Your global purpose may involve being a healer, teacher, writer, artist, comedian, or advocate for animals or children . . . or some other role.

This question is best relayed to Archangel Michael, who oversees everyone's life purpose. Fortunately, Michael is the loudest, bluntest, and clearest angel with whom to communicate. So, for life-purpose readings, focus upon your client's first name (remember the Power of the Name, as outlined in Chapter 3)

and the particular way in which the person worded the question. Meditate upon the energy of these words.

Notice and tell your client everything that comes to your mind and body in response to the query, even if you think you might be making it up or it might be intended for *you.* (*Note:* many times, the angel answers we give for others are also for ourselves, and this doesn't invalidate them.)

Most people want to know specific details and directions concerning their life purpose, so keep asking Archangel Michael for information and continue relaying it to your client. You'll gain confidence in doing life-purpose readings as your clients give you positive feedback after they've followed, and been successful due to, your readings' messages.

Romance Questions

The most common romance angel-reading question is: "Is this person my soul mate?" No one asks this unless there are doubts about the relationship. If someone is your soul mate, you don't need to ask anyone.

On the other hand, every romantic attachment happens for a purpose and is an opportunity to heal old emotional wounds (usually related to your parents). Romantic attraction functions like a laser, and you're drawn to people through whom you can forgive your dad or mom. While these "healing" relationships can be bumpy, they ultimately lead to huge spiritual growth for both people.

The best way to handle romantic questions is to use the Power of the Name. Ask your client for the first name of the romantic partner in question. Then meditate upon it until you begin to get impressions through your feelings, thoughts, visions, or words. Relay these impressions to your client.

During romance readings, it's extra important to be very conservative with your answers. If a longtime-married person or a woman with young children asks whether to get a divorce, for example, definitely explore alternatives such as marital counseling. When working with angels, you look for avenues that bring everyone peace whenever possible.

Health Questions

With health questions, the issue of free will frequently arises. For example, if your clients ask how their health will be in the future, you have the opportunity to teach about prayer, positive affirmations, and other considerations. Do some research on the latest studies about prayer's healing efficacy on the Internet or by reading a Larry Dossey book.

If you're guided to conduct spiritual healing during the reading, you can ask your client for permission to do so. This is entirely appropriate.

However, always keep your ethical considerations in mind when conducting a health reading. Stay conservative, and don't advise clients to stop seeing their medical doctor or give up their medications (although many times, getting a second opinion or checking with their physician about reducing or changing their prescriptions can be appropriate). My adage is: "If in doubt, refer out." In other words, if you've got a situation you're not sure about, refer the client to someone who specializes in that area.

It's also a good idea to meet local health practitioners who are spiritually minded, to engage in client referrals. You can meet spiritual professionals at churches and temples and at metaphysical bookstores.

Remote Readings

Your client doesn't have to be physically present with you during a reading. You can talk to anyone's guardian angels, regardless of location. Angel Therapy Practitioners regularly give professional readings via e-mail, letters, and over the telephone with the same effectiveness as if the session were in person.

To conduct a remote reading, simply imagine the person sitting or standing before you. Scan his or her head and shoulders for angels and energies, just as if the individual were physically beside you. Talk to the angels in the same fashion as if it were an in-person reading.

Most of all, trust the impressions that you receive, because they're just as real as in any other form of reading.

Any Other Questions?

You can answer any questions your clients pose by relaying these queries to the angels. Using these methods, you'll always receive valuable guidance to help your clients.

In the next chapter, we'll focus upon divination methods that can also yield detailed information for you and your clients.

CHAPTER 11

Oracle Cards and Other Divination Methods

When I first began giving angel readings, I used tarot cards as a supplemental tool to provide additional information during each session. I quickly discovered that some of the symbols, words, and images on the tarot cards frightened or worried some of my clients.

One morning I had a vivid lucid dream in which my grandmother Pearl (who frequently helps me from Heaven) said to me, "Study Pythagoras." I woke up with a start and said aloud, "The triangle guy?" To me, Pythagoras was a character from high school geometry class.

But since I highly respect Grandma Pearl's wisdom and guidance, I read every book and article I could find about the ancient

Greek philosopher and mathematician. I even discovered during a past-life regression that I was one of his students.

The details from that regression, combined with my research into Pythagorean teachings, showed me that the universe is numerically orderly and precise. Everything vibrates and is alive. So when you ask a question, the corresponding oracle card you choose is matching it and the situation's vibrations.

I was guided to create oracle cards based upon Pythagorean philosophy and tarot principles. These cards would have the same ancient wisdom as tarot without potentially frightening images or words. Since I worked with angels, it seemed natural to make my deck consist of "angel cards."

Hay House published them, with a positive reception. I really feel that creating oracle cards is part of my life purpose. After all, two indicators that you're aligned with your life purpose are: (1) feeling joy as you engage in the activity; and (2) doors opening for you easily while experiencing success with the service or product. If either of these elements is missing, then you can make adjustments just like you would when driving a car. When you're on the right road, these two factors are the journey *and* the destination.

Oracle cards can give you details about, and a basis for, the answers you receive during angel readings. Each deck of my oracle cards comes with a detailed guidebook with instructions on how to clear, consecrate, and spread out the cards. Everyone who uses them is equally able to give an accurate reading, and with practice you gain confidence in the cards.

Automatic Writing

The angelic messages in my book *Angel Therapy* were received through the process of "automatic writing." This is a method that allows you to record detailed messages from Heaven. You'll probably notice that your automatic-writing transmissions involve words that aren't a part of your normal vocabulary. You may find that your handwriting changes, and that you can suddenly spell words that you weren't able to before (and vice versa).

Automatic writing can also assist you on your spiritual path. For instance, through this method you can have conversations with God, your guardian angels, the ascended masters, and the archangels. You can ask your angels, "What are your names?" and other queries. And you can request that the archangels and ascended masters help you remember, and work on, your life purpose.

You can handwrite what you receive, or type it on a typewriter or word processor. If you're writing by hand, you'll need at least four pieces of regular-sized paper, a firm writing surface, and a reliable writing utensil. It's a great idea to have some soothing music playing in the background and to adopt a comfortable sitting position.

Begin your automatic-writing sessions with a prayer. The following is the one I use. It's based on my own spiritual faith, so you may want to rewrite it to fit *your* belief system. I would never tell anyone whom to pray to, but I do offer this prayer as an example of a way to effectively ask for help:

"Dear God, Holy Spirit, Jesus, Archangel Michael, all of my guides, and all of my angels, I ask that you watch over this automatic-writing session and ensure that anyone who comes through is a positive and loving being. Please boost my ability to clearly hear, see, conceptualize, and feel your Divine communication. Please help me accurately receive these messages and bring forth those that will carry blessings to me and to anyone who may read them. Thank you, and amen."

Then, think about whomever you wish to connect with in Heaven. Mentally ask that being to have a conversation with you.

You're going to pose a question and then write the response that you receive in a question-and-answer format, similar to an interview. The most important thing to keep in mind while doing automatic writing is to be completely authentic. Record whatever impressions you get, even if you're unsure whether it's your imagination or not. If you're getting nothing, write that down. You begin with jotting down whatever is occurring for you, and then eventually it switches over and becomes true spiritual communication.

During the automatic-writing session, you may feel as if someone else is controlling your pen or pencil. As I mentioned earlier, your handwriting, vocabulary, and spelling style will likely change during the session. Don't let this frighten you, as fear can block Divine communication. Remember, you're safe and protected by God and Archangel Michael (who is the "bouncer angel" and won't let any beings come near you unless they have loving intentions). Your hand may also start to doodle little circles, which is the spirit world's way of greeting you and saying, *"We're so happy to connect with you!"* If the doodling continues for too long, tell them, "I'm happy to connect, too, but would you please switch over to communication that I can understand?"

Your ego will probably have a field day during your automatic-writing session. It will scream that you're "just making this whole thing up!" If that happens, put the burden of proof that you're receiving authentic communications on the being with whom you're conversing. Ask the being, "How do I know that I'm not just making you up?" The answer will likely convince you of the authenticity of your Divine conversation. If you're still not certain, though, keep asking until you receive a message that puts your ego to rest. Or, ask the being to give you a physical sign, and then stop writing. Once you receive that sign, you'll feel more confident during your next session.

Now, let's begin by having you think of a query that you'd genuinely like answered. Mentally ask the spiritual being this question. Then, write it down at the top of the page while mentally repeating it. Be optimistic, holding the positive thought that you'll be answered.

Record whatever impressions you pick up through any of the four channels of Divine communication: thoughts, feelings, words, or visions. Then, ask another question and receive another answer . . . and so on.

When you're done writing to one being, you can switch to conversing with a different one. When your communications are complete, be sure to thank everyone involved.

The angels say that they love to give us messages, and that doing so is inherently rewarding to them because it's fulfilling God's will. Yet, when we thank our angels, our hearts fill with gratitude. And that warm feeling of appreciation is the "I love you" that we exchange with our celestial guardians as a fitting finish to a love letter from Heaven.

Practice asking your angels questions and then listening to their replies. In time, you'll learn to instantly distinguish the voice of the angels from that of ego. It's similar to picking up the telephone and immediately knowing whether it's a loved one or a solicitor who's calling. Also, with practice, you'll learn to trust and lean upon the angels' guidance as you experience successes by following their loving advice.

You can ask your angels to help you hear them better, or to understand the meaning of their more cryptic messages. Here are some other ways to increase the clarity of your Divine communication:

— **Breathe.** When you're stressed, you often hold your breath. This blocks you from hearing the messages that could *relieve* your stress. So, remember to breathe deeply when you're conversing with your angels. The angels have told me that their messages are carried upon the molecules of oxygen. So the more fresh air you take in, the louder their messages seem to be. That's why it's easier to hear your angels when you're outside in nature, or near water sources (including your shower or bathtub).

— **Relax.** Trying too hard prevents clear Divine communication. You needn't strain to hear your angels, as they're more motivated than you are to communicate. Instead, physically relax with your breath. Be in a receptive state, and ask your angels to help you release any tension in your mind or body.

— **Follow your guidance.** If your angels are asking you to improve your diet, it's probably because they know that processed foods and chemicals create static on the Divine communication lines. Your angels are your best teachers in guiding you as to how to better hear their voices. Ask for their assistance in this regard, and then follow whatever guidance you receive.

— **Ask for signs.** If you're unsure whether you're accurately hearing your angels, ask them to give you a sign. As always, it's best not to specify what type of sign you want. Allow the angels' infinite creativity to devise a wonderful one that you'll easily recognize. You'll delight in the loving sense of humor they display.

The angels give us signs so that we'll know that they and their messages are real. Signs can be anything that you see or hear in the physical world three or more times, or once in a very unusual way. For instance, if you hear the same book title from three or more different sources, then it's probably a recommendation from your angels to read that work.

The angels also leave us feathers in unusual places as a sign of their presence, probably because we associate feathers with angel wings. Another common sign is seeing angel-shaped clouds. Sometimes the signs we receive are fragrances, rather than something we see or hear. Many people report smelling perfume, flowers, or smoke when their angels are nearby.

Angel Lights

As I mentioned before, about 50 percent of my audience members worldwide report seeing flashes of light with their physical eyes. These lights look like camera flashbulbs or shimmering sparkles. Sometimes they're white; and other times they're bright jewel shades of purple, blue, green, and other colors. Several people have told me they had their eyes examined by ophthalmologists because they worried that their visions of sparkling lights were abnormal. Yet, the eye doctors told them that their physical eyes were perfectly healthy.

That's because these lights have *non*physical origins. I call this phenomenon "angel lights" or "angel trails." When you notice these, you're seeing the friction or energy of angels moving across the room. The white lights are from our guardian angels. Colorful ones originate from archangels.

Here's a list to help you know which archangels you're encountering when you see colored flashes or sparkles of light. (I've included a similar list in the Appendix of this book.)

- **Beige:** Azrael, the archangel who helps us heal from grief
- **Blue (aqua):** Raguel, who helps with relationships
- **Blue (dark):** Zadkiel, the archangel who helps us improve our memory and mental functioning
- **Blue (pale, almost white):** Haniel, who helps women with their feminine health, and assists with clairvoyance

- **Green (bright emerald):** Raphael, the healing archangel
- **Green (pale):** Chamuel, the archangel who helps us find whatever we're looking for
- **Green with dark pink:** Metatron, who helps children retain their spiritual gifts and self-esteem
- **Pink (bright fuchsia):** Jophiel, who helps us beautify our thoughts and life
- **Pink (pale):** Ariel, who helps with animals, nature, and manifestation
- **Purple (bright, almost cobalt blue):** Michael, who gives us courage and protection
- **Rainbow:** Raziel, who heals spiritual and psychic blocks and teaches us esoteric secrets
- **Turquoise:** Sandalphon, the musical archangel
- **Violet (reddish purple):** Jeremiel, who helps us heal our emotions
- **Yellow (dark):** Gabriel, who helps messengers and parents
- **Yellow (pale):** Uriel, the archangel of wisdom

Angel Numbers

Another common way in which the angels speak to us is by showing us number sequences. Have you ever noticed that when you look at the clock, a license plate, or a phone number, you see the same digits repeatedly? This is not a coincidence, but rather a message from above.

Since the era of Pythagoras, we've known that numbers carry powerful vibrations. Musical instruments and computers are based upon mathematical formulas, and the angels' number messages are just as precise.

The basic meaning of the numbers you see are:

0—You are loved by your Creator.

1—Watch your thoughts and only think about your desires instead of your fears, as you'll attract what you're thinking about.

2—Keep the faith and don't give up hope.

3—Jesus or other ascended masters are helping you.

4—The angels are assisting you with this situation.

5—A positive change is coming up for you.

6—Release any fears about the physical/material world to God and the angels. Balance your thoughts between the material and spiritual.

7—You're on the right path . . . keep going!

8—Abundance is coming to you now.

9—Get to work on your life's purpose without delay.

When you see a combination of numbers, simply "add" the meanings above together. For instance, if you see 428, this would mean: "The angels are with you, so keep the faith, as abundance is coming to you now."

The angels speak to us through many varied and creative means. If you *feel* that you're receiving their guidance, then you probably *are*. Ask your angels to help you recognize their signs and messages, and you'll begin to notice them all around you. The more you observe and follow these signs with success, the more confidence you'll have in the angels . . . and yourself.

CHAPTER 12

Angel Therapy Healing

The angels taught me these methods during my meditations and healing sessions. Everyone can use them effectively, from the very first attempt. . . .

Etheric Cord Cutting

Anyone who works with other people, either professionally or by offering unpaid acts of kindness, should know about etheric cords and how to handle them. Basically, whenever a person forms a fear-based attachment to you (such as being afraid that you'll leave, or believing that you are his or her source of energy or happiness), a cord is constructed between the two of you. This tie is visible to anyone who is clairvoyant, and palpable to anyone who is intuitive.

The cords resemble surgical tubing, and they function like gasoline hoses. When a needy person has formed an attachment to you, that person suctions energy from you through this etheric cord. You may not see it, but you can perceive its effect—namely, feeling tired or sad without knowing why. Well, it's because the person at the other end has just drawn on your power or sent you toxic energy through the cord.

Additionally, if you've got a cord to someone who's angry, then that fiery energy comes tumbling down it, straight into your body. This results in sharp, pinching pain without any organic cause.

So anytime you've helped someone—or whenever you feel lethargic, sad, or tired—it's a good idea to "cut your cords." If you've had relationships with perpetually angry people—or if you ever feel sharp pain—then it's time to employ this technique.

You aren't rejecting, abandoning, or "divorcing" the person by cutting these bonds. You're only severing the dysfunctional, fearful, codependent area of the relationship. The loving part of it remains attached.

To cut your own cords, say either mentally or aloud:

"Archangel Michael, I call upon you now. Please cut the cords of fear that are draining my energy and vitality. Thank you."

Then be silent for a few moments. Be sure to inhale and exhale deeply during the process, as breath opens the door for angels to help you. You'll probably feel cords being cut or pulled out of you. You may sense air-pressure changes or other tangible signs that the cord cutting is occurring.

The people on the other end will think of you without knowing why at the moment when their cords are being cut. You may even find that you get lots of "just thinking about you" phone messages and e-mails from those you were "attached" to. Don't buy into faulty beliefs about these people. Remember, *you* are not their source of energy or happiness—God is. The cords will grow back each time someone re-forms a fear-based attachment to you, so keep cutting them as needed.

You can also cut other people's fear-based cords by calling upon Archangel Michael to do so, or by detecting them yourself (you can see or feel cords by scanning the person's body with your spiritual sight and/or your hands).

Sometimes people may resist cutting cords to someone they resent. The persistent anger or desire for revenge can keep a toxic relationship tied to them. In those cases, not even Archangel Michael can cut the cords!

So you'll need to talk and walk your client through the individual cord-cutting procedure. As you discern each one, your intuition will tell you whom it is attached to. You may get a general impression ("I feel this cord is attached to a man") or more details ("This cord feels like it's attached to your father"). However it comes to you is fine. Just give your client whatever impressions you receive.

Then say to your client, "Please take some deep breaths and be willing to release old toxic energies related to _____ [name or title of person to whom the cord is attached]. Be willing to detoxify yourself so that you can enjoy peace, health, and happiness." Keep repeating this while supporting your client's process of deciding to let go of old anger. Sometimes this takes a while, but eventually everyone chooses reconciliation. Think of yourself as a shepherd of peace, gently and patiently coaxing your client in that direction.

Addiction Cord Cutting

This is a very effective method for reducing or eliminating cravings for addictive substances, as well as destructive behaviors. It can be used in conjunction with 12-step and other recovery

programs. You can use the following for yourself or read it aloud to another person:

Begin by thinking about any addictions that you feel completely ready to release. (This only works if you truly want to let go of them.) You can simultaneously choose and release as many as you want.

Next, imagine that the addictive items, or a symbol of the situation, are sitting on your lap. Notice the web of cords connecting them to your body, especially around your belly button. These are the attachments of fear, wherein you believe that you need these addictions.

Now call upon the archangels Michael and Raphael to dissolve these cords and cart away your addictions to Heaven, for transmutation and healing. Keep breathing, and hold the willingness to completely release these dependencies. Focus upon how wonderful you feel to be free of controlling cravings. Know how much more time, energy, money, and self-esteem you now have as a result of making this healthful decision.

Once you have felt a big release, Archangel Raphael will send his emerald green light through your severed cords. As you inhale deeply, you draw this healing energy into your body. <u>This</u> is actually what you have been craving, because it is God's love and light. That is really what you have been desiring, and trying to attain through your previous addictions. Drink in as much of Raphael's healing energy as you want, as there is an unlimited supply for you and everyone else. Any former emptiness or anxiety is now lifted away and you are at peace. Thank Raphael and Michael for this healing.

Vacuuming

When we worry about someone, blame ourselves for his or her misery, or massage someone who's in emotional pain, we may take on the other person's negative psychic energy in a misguided form of helpfulness. Everyone does this, especially lightworkers, who are ultra-concerned about aiding others—often at their own expense. The angels give us methods such as vacuuming to help us stay balanced in our service work. They want us to help people, but not to hurt ourselves in the process. It's a matter of being open to receiving support from others, including the angels. Many lightworkers are wonderful at giving aid, but not so good at receiving it. This is a method to help counterbalance that tendency.

To vacuum yourself with the help of the angels, mentally say, <u>Archangel Michael, I call upon you now to clear and vacuum the effects of fear.</u> In your mind, you'll then see or feel a large being appear—this is Archangel Michael. He will be accompanied by smaller angels known as the "Band of Mercy."

Notice that Michael is holding a vacuum tube. Watch as he puts it in through the top of your head (known as the "crown chakra"). You must decide whether you want the vacuum speed to be on extra-high, high, medium, or low. You'll also be directing him where to put the tube during the clearing process. Mentally guide it inside your head, in your body, and around all of your organs. Vacuum every part, all the way to the tips of your fingers and toes.

You may see or feel clumps of psychic dirt go through the vacuum tube, just like when you're cleaning a soiled carpet. Any entities that enter the vacuum are humanely treated at the other end by the Band of Mercy, who meets and escorts entities to the Light. Keep vacuuming until no more psychic debris goes through the tube.

As soon as you're clear, Archangel Michael will reverse the switch so that thick, toothpaste-like white light comes out of the tube. This is a form of "caulking" material that will fill in the spaces that formerly held psychic dirt.

Vacuuming is one of the most powerful techniques I've ever tried. You can also use this method on others, in person or remotely. Just hold the intention of working on them, and it's done! Even if you don't clearly see or feel anything during the process, or you worry, *Am I just making this up?* the results will be palpable. Most people see an immediate lifting of depression and a cessation of anger following a vacuuming session.

You can ask for a vacuum to be permanently installed above your head, in your home, at the office, or wherever you like. Think of it as an automatic filter, much like people have in their swimming pools. This permanent vacuum will ensure that you stay cleared at all times.

Lifting the Energy of Psychic Attack

Occasionally, when people are angry at themselves or someone else, they send toxic energy that can create physical pain in their target. This is called a "psychic attack." Sometimes these assaults happen deliberately, and sometimes they're unintentional.

To lift these toxic energies from yourself or another, first call upon Archangel Michael and Archangel Raphael. Then either lie on your stomach or move forward in your chair so your back isn't touching anything. You can read the following aloud as a guided healing meditation for yourself or for another person's benefit:

As you breathe deeply, be willing to release any old anger energy from your back, shoulders, neck, and other areas of your

body. Breathe, and feel or see the energy forms (which often look like daggers, arrows, and other instruments of attack) lift from your body.

As these instruments easily float out of your back and body, you may get the sense of who sent them to you. Do your best to hold compassion for the person and resist any temptation to retaliate. Ask the angels to send healing energies to both of you, to break the cycle of attack. Keep breathing and lifting the old energy out of your body. You may feel quivers and shivers as each instrument is carried away by the angels.

When your body feels calm and peaceful, you see Archangel Raphael kneeling beside you. He is sending his emerald green healing energy around and into your body. This light instantly heals any incisions where attack instruments were formerly lodged, restoring your body to its true natural state of wholeness. Archangel Michael seals you in his protective purple light, which also deflects any subsequent lower energies. You are now cleared and protected!

Healing Past-Life Vows

You may have taken vows in your past lives as a spiritual aspirant or devotee (such as a nun or a monk). Among the most common are vows of suffering, self-sacrifice or retribution, poverty, virginity, chastity/celibacy, obedience, and silence. Unless these vows are severed, they can follow you to Earth and place barriers in your love and sexual areas, finances, and life in general. No one is truly free until these past-life commitments are broken. The only healthy vows are those that *you* decide upon—the ones you make with yourself. Even then, you'll want to regularly review them to see if they're still valid.

Release these vows and their effects by calling upon Archangel Raziel, who helps us to heal the vestiges of past lifetimes. Then, on your own behalf or to help another person, strongly affirm:

"Archangel Raziel, I ask for your help; and I hereby sever any vows of suffering, self-sacrifice, or retribution that I may have made, in all directions of time. I rescind any negative effects of these vows, now and forever."

Then, repeat this statement for other vows (poverty, celibacy, and so on).

The angels and archangels will guide you through additional healing methods, or adjust and supplement the ones outlined in this chapter. Trust these intuitive messages, as Heaven teaches you to gain confidence in your natural healing abilities.

PART III

You Are a Spiritual Teacher and Healer

CHAPTER 13

Lightworkers and Your Life Purpose

Before we dive into the question "Can I support myself and my family financially with a spiritually based career?" (and by the way, the short answer is: "Absolutely yes!"), let's cover some background topics.

First, I believe that each person has a personal mission in life—something that you agreed to learn during this lifetime. It could be patience, forgiveness, compassion, balance, self-care, integrity, and so forth. Everyone is working on a soul-growth lesson.

In addition to their personal missions, some individuals agreed to take on "global missions," which involve helping people, animals, the environment, or a cause other than themselves. Not everyone has a global mission. Some people on Earth are only living for their own personal growth.

Those who have global missions are known as *lightworkers*.

This is a name I'm using that encompasses similar terms such as *Indigo, Crystal,* and *Earth Angel.*

You know you're a lightworker if you feel compelled to help others, and deeply care about the world. You attract people who need help, and you're sensitive to the needs of those around you. In fact, you sometimes feel that you're a bit too sensitive, as you absorb energies from others' moods. But don't worry—we'll discuss shielding and other energy-protection methods later.

As a lightworker, you've always felt a sense of purpose, as if there's something important that you're destined to do in this lifetime. You may not know what this destiny entails, but you can feel it. All lightworkers do.

There's even a sense of time urgency associated with this, like an alarm clock ringing in the pit of your gut, urging you to *go, go, go* and make a positive difference in the world. These feelings are universal among lightworkers.

The great news is that, as a lightworker, you've been making a positive difference your entire life. You radiate healing energy that soothes others and brings peace wherever you go. That's because your main global purpose is to love, which is something you do naturally. You care about people; and you wish that everyone could be happy, healthy, and well provided for. You are a giver.

So, the *form* that your mission takes is secondary as long as you extend Divine love. In other words, when you think about a career as a spiritual teacher or healer, the type of work you do isn't important. Whether you teach or practice Reiki, Angel Therapy, mediumship, or some other modality . . . if it's done from a place of loving service, everything else is details.

With that in mind, there's a practical consideration when deciding on a teaching or healing modality. You're forming a long-term relationship with your chosen field, so please make sure it's an area that truly excites and interests you. It's not smart to select one just because you've seen another person gain material success by that avenue.

Whatever type of healing or teaching you choose, please be certain that you love it. I've watched lightworkers create career goals with their heads, using business plans and projections, only to meet with one obstacle after another because their hearts weren't in the work. And while planning and projecting can be helpful and prudent starting points for new business ventures, make sure that you're leading with your heart.

In spiritually based careers, your feelings and intuition are your road map. Your head is second in charge, as the employee of your heart.

So what topic—even if it seems illogical—really excites you? Let's ask your higher self:

Take a moment to relax in a quiet place, either lying down or sitting. Close your eyes if possible, and give yourself full permission to dream about your ideal career. Then notice what images, thoughts, and feelings come to you:

- *Are you working alone, with a co-worker, or with several co-workers?*
- *Do you operate from home, out of a healing center, or where?*
- *What type of clients or students are you involved with?*
- *How do you feel about this work?*

As you allow yourself to imagine your ideal career, notice how warm and fulfilled you feel. These feelings are the ultimate paycheck, the greatest reward. And as you feel satisfied, your material benefits are drawn to you by the Law of Attraction.

Faith and Confidence

Your dream of having a full-time career as a spiritual teacher or healer is much more than a dream. It's a *sign.* If you continually imagine yourself having a meaningful career that supports you and your family financially, emotionally, and spiritually, then this is a sign that your life purpose involves this type of work.

And yet it's not enough to dream. Action is required. However, it isn't that simple, is it? Otherwise you'd already be on your way.

Lightworkers are, by definition, sensitive. They're receptive to the energies in any room they walk into. They're attuned to other people's moods and feelings and to environmental factors such as chemicals, pollution, or noise. They're conscious of the presence of angels.

And they're also sensitive to other people's opinions. This sensitivity is both a gift and a lifesaving instinct. You see, your overall personality remains fairly constant throughout lifetimes. Once a lightworker, always a lightworker.

You've been a spiritual teacher or healer many, many times before in other lives. You've been a priest or priestess, temple-keeper, monk or nun, alchemist, sorcerer or sorceress, seer, scribe, astronomer, or other form of esoteric healer and teacher (or maybe all of the above!).

Yet, although there have always been lightworkers on this planet, they weren't always treated kindly. History is rife with tales of witch trials and inquisitions during Earth's dark ages (those periods of time when the physical and tangible are accorded more respect than the nontangible and spiritual).

It's been historically common for people, governments, and churches to blame lightworkers for plagues, bad crop years, and other calamities. So to stay alive and avoid punishment, lightworkers have developed an ultra-sensitivity to other people's approval or disapproval. (Plus, they want everyone to be happy.)

We'll discuss how to develop healthy assertiveness and boundaries later. But for now it's important to recognize your natural tendencies that some might call "people pleasing," but which I see as instinctive survival skills, combined with the sensitivity that underlies all psychic abilities.

These qualities also arise when you're teased about your lightworker characteristics. If you've been called "weird," "odd," "too sensitive," or worse, then you've experienced mild forms of the ostracizing that lightworkers have historically undergone. That's why many lightworkers tend to isolate. Think of the wizard living alone in the woods and you get the picture.

Yet in modern-day society, isolating isn't very practical. Most people have to work with others out of necessity and emotional need. If you find interacting with your peers difficult, then you're likely socializing and working in harsh environments. Once you make the switch to a spiritually based career, you'll find welcome relief as you become surrounded by other sensitive and gentle people.

Coming Out of the Spiritual Closet

Many lightworkers hesitate to become public healers and teachers because of fears of further teasing, rejection, or ostracism. *What will people think?* the lightworker anxiously asks. This is especially true if their families hold traditional religious values or are conservative.

I call this process "coming out of the spiritual closet," where you reveal your true beliefs to others. I wouldn't recommend holding a debate about spirituality or religion, because no one is converted through fear or anger. Instead, let your "outing" happen gradually and naturally. Perhaps you begin by mentioning a spiritual book that you've enjoyed reading, and then go from there.

Remember: you aren't out to be a spiritual teacher to your loved ones unless they voluntarily ask for such lessons. You and your family are going through spiritual-growth lessons already in this lifetime just by learning to function peacefully with one another.

The truth is that some people *will* judge or criticize you as you become publicly known for your spiritual work. Something about spirituality just seems to bring out opinionated people.

The way I've dealt with this scrutiny is by reminding myself that there are *no* people in the spotlight who have been universally loved and accepted, because every public figure has also had detractors and persecutors.

So expecting everyone to like you and your work is unrealistic. Accept that you'll attract the people who are supposed to work with you, and let the rest go. Forgive your critics and judges, as they're just afraid to spend their time on their own life purpose (if they were doing so, they'd be too busy to condemn others). As you feel compassion for them, the sting of their words will lessen.

The Law of Attraction also operates in this vein. If you fear criticism or judgment, you'll definitely attract more of it.

I love the adage of Alcoholics Anonymous: "When you judge me, you've got one finger pointed at me, and three pointed back at yourself." This speaks to the *projection* aspect of judgment: *What you see in me is something you see in yourself.*

My favorite book, *A Course in Miracles,* says that our fear-based egos hide from our conscious awareness. We don't want to see the darkness within them, so we project awareness outward by seeing it in others. A wonderful clearing affirmation that the angels gave me years ago is great to recite whenever you feel angry at someone: "I am willing to release that part of me that irritates me when I think of you."

A Course in Miracles also says that guilt attracts negative experiences, because this emotion always expects punishment. So be sure to enter your spiritually based career with excitement and a clear conscience. Don't hide what you're doing behind people's backs, because this will create an unhealthy energy ripple that will attract what you most fear: being discovered. Instead, just go about your work unapologetically and trust the Law of Attraction to bring you exactly the right students, audiences, and clients . . . because it will!

Remember: You already *are* a spiritual teacher and healer. You were born one, and you've been practicing your art for lifetimes.

For example, if you've been attracting strangers who tell you their life stories and problems, you've been using your hands to heal people's ailments, or you've been counseling your girlfriends through their life crises, then yes, you're already working as a spiritual teacher and healer.

Now it's time to get paid for it.

Oops, did that sentence create a blip in your consciousness just now? My apologies. However, I actually did want you to get in touch with this feeling because it's essential to moving forward.

You see, in order to be a *professional* spiritual teacher or healer, you must allow yourself to be compensated. How else are you going to quit your day job and support yourself, if you don't allow your clients and students to pay you?

If this idea makes you uncomfortable, then let's explore the reasons, because—unhealed—this could be a major block to the development of your career.

First, how do you feel about people accepting money for spiritually based actions? If you hold an idealistic sense of altruism, a belief that we should freely give that which God gave to us, I totally understand your feelings. And if you have other sources of income that still allow you enough time to focus upon your spiritual teaching and healing work, then wonderful! Feel free to give away your spiritual offerings as you are guided to.

For many people, volunteer work and selfless service are the foundations of personal spiritual growth. And I got my first job as a counselor after volunteering at a hospital for several months, so there are also practical benefits to donating your time.

Those who abhor the idea of accepting payment for spiritual work are likely recalling past lifetimes when they lived in communal settings such as a lamasery (a monastery of lamas) or monastery. In those lifetimes, your food and shelter were provided for. You were free to focus upon your spiritual path without regard for earning an income.

But in modern times, we usually need a salary to pay our bills. You don't live in a communal setting; and you're responsible for your utilities, mortgage, and groceries. You likely have a job right now that pays your bills. The question is: do you *love* your job?

I believe that we're meant to work in jobs that bring us and others joy. We're meant to have careers that are personally meaningful, which we feel good about. And when we love our work, everything else (like getting paid) naturally falls into place.

When you love what you do, your primary focus isn't money based; it's love based. Yet, you still make money, because this is the natural order of giving and receiving.

Since I began teaching my Angel Therapy Practitioner class in 1996, I've watched graduates and their careers. A clear pattern has emerged of three types of approaches to a spiritually based career, with corresponding results:

1. **Using one's head, not one's heart.** I've seen people with business backgrounds approach spiritual teaching like a horse race, figuring odds and calculating returns. They buy expensive

advertisements and rent fancy ballrooms to hold events . . . and no one attends. Ouch, what happened?

Well, your potential students and clients are sensitive, just like you are. They can feel the intentions behind your workshops and healing practices. If your primary motive is riches or fame, then no one will be attracted to your work. Of course it's fine to make money from your spiritual work, but it can't be your *main* focus. If you need income while you're building your healing practice, then keep your day job for a while or take on a part-time job and gradually ease into self-employment.

2. **Feeling too timid to try.** This situation may seem like the opposite of the one above, but they have a lot in common because both come from fear. In the first scenario, the people use their heads to make decisions about their spiritually based careers because deep down they don't trust their intuition and personal desires. They may have ego-based competitive drives, too. And those who are too timid to step out and follow their intuition are plagued by low self-confidence or indecisiveness . . . which usually means the fear of making the wrong move or decision.

However, there's a little-known universal law that is in operation always: the Law of Action. This rule states that as you take *any* action in the direction of your goal—no matter how seemingly small—the universe will take an even greater step in *your* direction to meet and support your goal.

So if you have a dream to be a spiritual teacher or healer, then do something about it . . . now! You'll read specific ideas and examples of steps to take a bit later.

3. **Taking guided action.** Taking action requires faith and guts, for sure. That's why I qualify this category by saying it's "guided" action, which means following your intuition.

One of my favorite quotes is from the author Sheldon Kopp: "I've never begun any important venture for which I felt adequately prepared." This statement speaks to the fact that the ego will always try to con you into believing that you're not ready to take action. It will tell you that because you don't *feel* prepared, you *aren't* prepared.

The ego also uses a ploy called the "impostor phenomenon," in which it tells you that you're unqualified, a fake, or a phony. This is extremely common, especially among intelligent and successful people. It's based upon the old energy that says you have to suffer and work extremely hard to get anything worthwhile. So if things come easily (as they often do for intelligent people), then your ego says it can't be valuable or real. Once you recognize that these feelings aren't based upon reality, then they can no longer thwart you.

A woman enrolled in my Angel Therapy Practitioner course with the clear intention that she'd graduate and immediately begin a full-time career giving angel readings. She'd even rented an office and printed business cards prior to taking the course! And sure enough, as soon as she returned home after graduation, her private practice was successful in every sense of the word. She followed her intuition and took guided action.

People pay good money for business leads, yet the greatest source of professional guidance is free of charge: it's in your gut feelings. Spend time alone with yourself daily, listening to your intuition, and then take action accordingly. Your gut feelings are your best business partners.

Giving and Receiving Are Equally Important

When you give a reading or conduct a counseling session, workshop, or other helpful offering, it's only right that you receive something in exchange. Giving and receiving are equally important energies, and both are required for a balanced life.

Lightworkers are natural givers and caretakers. It's in our souls, instincts, and DNA to help others to feel happier and healthier. So we don't want to block or fight this inclination.

However, it's vital to balance all that giving with an equal measure of receiving. You may be uncomfortable receiving, because the ego makes you feel:

- **Obligated:** "If you give something to me, then I owe you."
- **Unneeded:** "As long as I'm the one doing the giving, then I'm needed. But if you give to me, then *I* need *you.*"
- **Out of control:** "I can control myself and my actions, but I can't control you if you're giving to me."
- **Guilty:** "I don't feel worthy of receiving from you."
- **Passive-aggressive:** "I don't want to give you the satisfaction of pleasing me."

These (usually unconscious) ego-based feelings and fears can stem from past lifetimes where you played the role of servant or slave or were otherwise controlled. Usually, however, these blocks stem from listening to the ego, which is all about fear, and its under-the-radar plan is to keep you from remembering your Divine identity and life purpose. The ego wants to keep you and others afraid and insecure, because that's its foundation and lifeblood.

Fortunately, you don't have any reason to listen to the ego's blather, because your higher self (who is one with God) is that part of you that performs the spiritual services you're offering. Your higher self already is a spiritual teacher, healer, lightworker, and so forth.

You express pure Divine love, wisdom, and creativity through your higher self, like a clear prism on a sunny day.

If you only give and don't allow yourself to receive, you'll feel burned-out and drained. You'll also be resentful, because deep down, you'll wish that others would guess your needs and fulfill them. This isn't fair in relationships, though. You've got to tell people what is important to you. If they're unresponsive to your needs and you've clearly outlined what they are, well, then it's time to rethink that relationship.

Giving is a masculine energy, and receiving is a feminine energy. As discussed in my book *Divine Magic,* both are needed in a well-balanced life. Besides, receiving and feminine energy are the basis of psychic awareness. To hear the Divine messages, you've got to be receptive. Otherwise, it's like having a conversation where no one is listening.

Every day, practice giving and receiving at least three times. When someone offers to help you, smile and say, "Yes, please" or "Thank you." Give any guilt or other harsh emotions to God and the angels. The exception would be if you get a strong gut feeling not to interact with a particular person. Always follow your gut.

When your clients or students pay you, similarly just say, "Thank you," and write them a receipt. Please don't talk about your discomfort or guilt about accepting money. Save that conversation for God and your guardian angels, who can reassure you and heal your feelings.

By accepting payment for your services, you are performing an "energy exchange," where the *giving* you just expended is balanced by *receiving* payment. Your clients or students will appreciate your services even more, since they exchanged something of value in order to receive them.

You are no different from other healers who accept payment, such as doctors or nurses (which are also sacred professions like yours).

As you put a price on your services, you are supported in important ways. The money allows you to devote more time to your healing and teaching practice. If you don't accept it, then you'll have to spend valuable time at a job to earn it . . . and this is time that you could use instead in service to your students, clients, and God.

Your past lifetime where you stood with a begging bowl is over. Today, you are a professional who deserves remuneration for your work. Remember that God answers prayers through people. Your students and clients who want to pay you for your work are part of the answer to your prayers. Just say "Yes" and "Thank you," as you allow yourself to receive.

High Self-Esteem Equals Confidence

The fastest way to increase your confidence and courage is to clean up your act, to put it bluntly. This means taking an inventory of any behaviors you currently engage in that you don't feel good about. Look at your diet, relationships, business practices, honesty with self and others, lifestyle, and other factors. Do any of your activities make you cringe? Do you engage in something that you hope no one discovers? Anything that makes you feel ashamed or guilty?

All of these deeds lower your self-esteem, which then lowers your confidence. Confidence comes from trusting your own self. It means having a great, trustworthy relationship with *you.* Because although you may be able to sneak behaviors past others, *you* know that you're engaging in them. And this makes you trust yourself less. All of which takes a toll on your confidence and self-esteem.

Just as you love someone who takes good care of you, so do you love yourself more when you take good care of *yourself*.

You can ask God and the angels for help (especially the healing angel, Raphael, and the angel of courage, Michael) in releasing cravings for unhealthful behaviors and addictions. Heaven can eliminate or reduce cravings so that you won't be tempted.

Sometimes we engage in unhealthful behaviors out of self-punishment because of underlying guilt. Well, this is a catch-22, circular situation because these activities then increase these feelings of guilt. We can break the cycle by calling upon spiritual assistance. (You can also get help with my free video on YouTube called "Healing of Addictions with Archangel Raphael.")

Unhealthful behaviors can also be procrastination tools or "delay tactics," for those afraid to move forward with their goals and priorities. Fears of failure *and* of success are real confidence-robbers that can lead to paralyzing indecision. I know—I've been there!

Since it's upsetting to procrastinate, it's easier to fool yourself by becoming busy with time-wasting activities such as addictions. For instance, when I wanted to write my first book, I felt intimidated by the process. So I made myself busy by becoming a perfectionistic housekeeper. I wanted my home to be immaculately clean before I'd allow myself the time to write. And of course, no home is ever immaculately clean, so I had the "perfect" excuse to perpetually procrastinate.

And I've used other delay tactics as well, including overeating (it takes *lots* of time to plan, prepare, eat, and then clean up after a meal), time-consuming relationships, and drinking wine, which zapped my energy and made me too tired to write.

Another delay tactic was to spend all my time on the phone with a girlfriend who had endless drama yet really didn't want advice, guidance, or help. She just wanted to complain. But for a

while I put my writing on hold in order to be there for her . . . for hours and days at a time.

At first, I resented her for taking so much of my time in a one-sided relationship (she never wanted to hear how my day was). Then I realized that I was using her as much as she was using me. I used her as a delay tactic to avoid writing, and she used me as a sounding board. After this realization, our "friendship" just naturally fizzled away.

Taking steps toward your dream feels like a giant leap into the unknown. By acting, you are committing to something that's super-important to you. It's a dream that you've kept in your back pocket for a long time, so it can feel threatening to actually look at it and work on it. I totally understand!

That's why it's a relief to realize that the development of your aspiration won't require a lot of your time. Investing even 30 minutes daily, taking *any* action step related to your dream, will rapidly propel your manifestations.

If you can dream it, you can do it!

CHAPTER 14

Action Steps to Take Right Now

As we've discussed, the universe positively responds to action that you take related to your dream. It doesn't matter what the step is or whether it's something major, minor, large, or small. The universe responds to *intentions,* and your efforts are a declaration of your objective to be a professional spiritual teacher and healer. Each time you take an action step, beautiful sparks shower the universe . . . sparks of faith, trust, confidence, and crystal clear intentions. These sparks have a life force, which creates *new* life.

So you needn't worry that you'll take the "wrong" action step, because everything counts and adds up in positive ways. In fact, you can rely on the universe to surprise you with undreamed-of opportunities . . . and the genesis of those opportunities begins with your intention and action steps.

Any action you take will open doors for you. So do something every single day related to your dream.

Always choose your actions based upon your intuition's directives, as your gut feelings are directly tied in to God's universal wisdom. Haven't you noticed that you always regret it when you ignore your gut feelings? Most people do. Hopefully, though, these experiences have helped you trust your intuition. And truly there's no need for regret, because we learn a great deal from so-called mistakes.

As you take action, please don't outline *how* you want your dreams to manifest. Simply put your whole focus upon this moment right now, and perform the action as you're guided. Let go of any worry about results or outcome. Trust the universe to process the strides you make and give you a desirable result.

Here are examples of significant action steps to take. Choose one or more a day, according to your intuitive guidance:

- Read a book or article related to your career topic.
- Make an appointment with a mentor (someone successful in your chosen field) to help you learn the business and to encourage you.
- Make a Vision Board, which is a large poster board or piece of construction paper on which you draw or paste pictures or words related to your dreams.
- Join or start a writers' group.
- Visualize yourself succeeding in your chosen profession.
- Write a paragraph or more for your article or book.
- Send query letters to literary agents, publishers, or magazines.

- Attend a class or seminar relevant to your field.
- Research speaking venues.
- Find and rent office space for your private practice.
- Create business cards or flyers for your work.
- Design and place an advertisement (most publications will help you with design).
- Pray and ask for help, support, and guidance.
- Visit a location that will yield new information for you.
- Join a networking group.

And here's some hard-won advice on what *not* to do: *please* don't share your dream with naysayers, skeptics, or negative people. There's too high a risk that their criticism will wipe the enthusiasm right out of you.

Your dream is like a newborn hummingbird, very fragile and precious. Hold it close to your chest, and only share it with loving and supportive people. Even then, I'd wait until the bird was strong enough to fly on its own.

Even the most supportive individuals may feel jealous or threatened as you discuss your dream. After all, they have dreams of their own. And if you're following yours and they're not . . . well, it brings up insecurities for some: *Will you get successful and leave me?* is a common one. And they may unconsciously sabotage you, without realizing they're doing so.

For right now, share your dream with yourself, God, and your angels. As it grows stronger, you can begin to give hints about it to others. But not yet. For now, just nurture it with positive thinking, prayer, and daily action steps.

The Archangels and Careers

The archangels are available to happily help you with all aspects of your career. Here are some of the roles that specific archangels fulfill in this area:

— **Ariel.** This archangel helps those interested in environment-, nature-, or animal-related careers. Ariel also aids in the manifestation of money or other supplies needed for your life purpose and day-to-day expenses.

— **Azrael.** If your career involves grief counseling or guiding people through losses (such as working at a hospital, hospice service, counseling center, or the like), this archangel can guide your words and actions to comfort and empower the bereaved.

— **Chamuel.** The "finding archangel" will help you locate the career or job you're seeking. Chamuel will also help you retain your peace of mind.

— **Gabriel.** The messenger archangel helps teachers, journalists, writers, and those who want to work with children. If you feel guided to write, Gabriel will motivate and direct you. If you'd like to help children in some way, ask Gabriel for a Divine assignment.

— **Haniel.** The archangel of grace is wonderful to invoke when going for a job interview, during meetings, or anytime you want to be extra-articulate and graceful.

— **Jophiel.** The archangel of beauty helps keep the energy clean and high at your workplace and your thoughts about your career positive. She also assists artists, creative types, anyone involved in the beauty business, and feng shui practitioners with all aspects of their professions.

— **Metatron**. If your career involves adolescents or energetic children, Metatron can help you. He can give you a Divine assignment if you'd like to work with teenagers. Metatron is also a wonderful motivator and organizer, so call upon him if you need assistance with your get-up-and-go drive.

— **Michael.** Archangel Michael can help you discern your life's purpose and the next step to take in your career. One of the best ways to call upon him is to write him a letter, inquiring about your best professional or educational choices. Michael is one of the loudest archangels, so you probably won't have any trouble hearing him. Write his replies below your questions in your letter so you have a record of his career guidance.

Michael's speaking style is to the point. He's very loving, but he's also very blunt. For this reason, he's a wonderful archangel to call upon for the courage to change or improve your career. He'll help you transition to a better job; begin your own business; and speak your truth lovingly to co-workers, bosses, and clients.

Michael is also amazing at fixing electronic and mechanical items such as computers, cars, fax machines, and such.

— **Raguel.** If your work involves relationships with clients and co-workers or mediation (such as marriage counseling), Archangel Raguel can ensure harmonious interactions.

— **Raphael.** If you're in a healing career or feel inclined to be a healer, Raphael can help you. As the chief healing angel, Raphael assists with all aspects of your vocation. Raphael can help you select the modality that you'd most enjoy, manifest tuition for your education, open and run a healing center, find the best employment in this field or start a successful private practice, and guide you toward expressing the most beneficial actions and words during your healing sessions.

— **Sandalphon.** This archangel helps with careers in the arts, especially music. Call upon Sandalphon as a muse to inspire you, a teacher to guide your creative process, and an agent to market your creative projects.

— **Uriel.** The archangel of light can illuminate your mind with wise ideas. Call upon Uriel for problem solving, brainstorming, or important conversations.

— **Zadkiel.** This archangel helps you improve your memory; and he's a wonderful helpmate for students or anyone who needs to remember names, figures, or other important information.

Zeroing in on Your Spiritual Path

Now it's time to decide on some specifics related to your work as a spiritual teacher and healer. You'll need to define your niche somewhat so that clients and students will know what you're offering. Don't worry—you don't need to label yourself into a corner. You'll be able to flex and breathe as you gradually discover what works for you.

Let's begin by looking at your hobbies: What do you like to do for fun in your spare time? While this may not become the basis of your career, it yields valuable clues as to your temperament and likes.

For instance, do you prefer to . . .

- . . . be indoors or outdoors?
- . . . be alone, with one special person or pet, or with a group of people?
- . . . have structure and know what's expected of you, or invent things as you go in a free-flowing style?

- . . . be involved with logical facts or artistic and creative ventures?
- . . . have supervision and someone showing you what to do, or be your own leader?
- . . . work part-time or full-time?
- . . . travel or stay home?
- . . . have a company provide health insurance and other employee benefits for you, or would you be comfortable paying for this yourself?
- . . . have a steady paycheck you can count on, or constantly manifest your income as you go along?

Answer these questions candidly, because your natural preferences are important considerations. It doesn't work to try to reinvent yourself to fit into a new career paradigm. Go with what you know are your definite likes and avoid your dislikes as you create your spiritual teaching and healing career.

It's important that you're blissful, thrilled, and excited about your new career venture. And a big part of your joy comes from creating conditions that are comfortable for you, including all of the preceding factors.

Choosing Your Focus

Okay, so you're all ready to write your book or article, give a speech, or start your healing practice. Congratulations!

The next question that I have for you is: "What's your topic?" or "What's your focus?"

In other words, it's not enough to say, "I want to teach or write." Actually, that's a good starting point, but it invites the question of what your topic is.

Before you shut this book and run away because my questions are pressing your buttons, please breathe and stay with me for a while. Everything is okay, I promise. You can do this.

As we discussed earlier, it's important to choose a topic that naturally excites you. This excitement will give you the enthusiasm necessary to propel you forward each day. If you don't like where you've focused your efforts, you'll avoid it. And that adds up to procrastination.

You can discern which topic naturally excites you by monitoring your conversations. Notice what piques your interest and causes you to speak faster or longer. And when you browse books or articles, which ones grab your attention? This is an important clue.

Also, notice your natural inclinations and trends with people. For example, do people tend to ask you for the same sort of help or information? If you already have a private practice, notice the patterns of questions that people pose to you. They're asking you to teach them about this topic.

Here are some categories to help you brainstorm, spark new ideas, and narrow down your interests:

- Addiction recovery
- Angels
- Animals and pets
- Arts and crafts
- Astrology
- Chanting and toning
- Children's issues
- Color therapy
- Crystal children
- Crystals and minerals
- Dance
- Domestic-violence prevention and recovery
- Dream interpretation
- Ecology and going green
- Energy healing
- Fairies
- Feng shui
- Flower essences
- Gluten-free diets
- Grief support
- Herbology
- Hermetics
- Homelessness and people in need
- Indigenous spiritual practices
- Indigo children
- Investing ethically
- Life coaching
- Manifestation and the Law of Attraction
- Massage and bodywork
- Mediumship
- Men's issues
- Mermaids
- Music
- Natural beauty products
- Numerology
- Nutrition
- Ocean protection
- Oracle cards
- Organization and time management
- Pilates
- Power places
- Psychic development
- Raw-food preparation
- Romance and relationships
- Sacred geometry
- Stress management
- Tai chi
- Unicorns
- Women's issues
- World religion and spirituality
- Writing and publishing
- Yoga

If you have a personal challenge that you've faced and have recovered from (like addiction or abuse issues), and it excites you to think about helping others through your life experience . . . this is a sign. Choose what truly excites you and brings you joy.

Use your heart, not your head, to make these decisions, because you'll be living with this topic for a while.

"Am I Ready?"

Once you choose a topic, are you immediately ready to begin teaching about it? The answer is: *Maybe.* Your higher self and intuition will tell you whether you need additional research, education, or preparation.

When I was guided to become a healer, I got very strong and clear guidance to return to college and study psychology. I loved this topic, so the classes were fun for me, even though they involved a lot of time and work.

I went back to school because of love, joy, and inner guidance. This is a positive example of preparation for a spiritually based career.

I've met other people, though, who attended school as a delay tactic so that they could procrastinate taking definitive action toward the realization of their dream. For them, education was motivated by fear instead of love.

One woman whom I worked with held three Ph.D.'s. Upon examining why, she realized that she was trying to feel adequate and qualified—and to win her father's approval—by collecting diplomas. Her realization helped her to move forward with her true dreams.

So if you're thinking of getting additional training, the salient question is: *Will this schooling delay me from taking action toward my dream?* If the answer is *no,* then the schooling likely originates from your higher self's wisdom. You'll know that it *definitely* does if it makes you feel happy.

It's possible to work concurrently on your dream and attend school. When I was earning my bachelor's degree in counseling psychology from Chapman University, I began volunteering at a

CareUnit drug- and alcohol-dependency treatment center. Within months, they hired me full-time. And while I learned valuable lessons at Chapman, my greatest schooling came from my hands-on work as a counselor. I *highly* recommend doing a volunteer internship in your chosen field with someone who's already established. You'll gain invaluable experience.

The ego will try to tell you that you're never ready to be a spiritual teacher, writer, or healer. That's because, as we discussed previously, it wants everyone to swim in a sea of fear and insecurity . . . which is the food of the ego.

I remember feeling very insecure when, as a counselor, I began teaching about, and helping people with, eating disorders. After all, I was newly in recovery from my own eating disorder. I was so anxious about my qualifications that I lost sleep over this issue.

But fortunately, I quickly discovered that as a "newbie," I had insight into what it felt like to be fresh upon the recovery path. I knew what it was like to release an addiction, because I'd just done so myself!

Sure, there are valuable experiences to be gained as a seasoned veteran. But those who have taught about a topic for many years probably have forgotten what it feels like to be newly on the path. And *that's* what novice teachers and healers can uniquely offer to their clients.

The Law of Attraction is ready to bring the right students and clients to you, as soon as you make the clear declaration that you are a spiritual healer, teacher, or writer (or all of the above).

Your crystal clear decision that you are *now* the embodiment of your career choice is more important than business cards, advertisements, or flyers. Don't make the mistake of seeing yourself as being in a spiritually based business *someday.* That type of visualization will always ensure that your dreamed-of career lies in the future, instead of in the present.

See, feel, think, and speak of yourself as being in your career of choice, right now. And while you're at it, please visualize and feel every other desired element as being true for you right now: financial security, a wonderful love life, vibrant health, high energy and motivation, a sense of meaning in your life, great friendships, successful projects, and so forth. See and feel everything you desire, as if it were a current event. *This* is how you draw it all rapidly into your life, in fabulously mysterious ways.

So write and affirm . . .

- "I *am* a spiritual teacher!"
- "I *am* a spiritual healer!"
- "I *am* a successful author!"

. . . and any other declarations of your desired career. Affirmations and visualization are powerful, and you're already using them—sometimes without realizing it! When you say, "Someday I'd like to . . ." you're affirming that your desire is in the future. Be sure that all of your declarations are in the present tense (even if you feel like you're just pretending). By repeatedly stating, "I *am* a spiritual teacher, now," the universe supports this statement with relevant experiences.

You can do it—you already *are!*

CHAPTER 15

Putting Yourself Out There

Not only will you be putting yourself out there before the public, you'll also be putting yourself "out there" spiritually, emotionally, and intellectually. I mean, it's a stretch to talk publicly about your beliefs. It's also a risk . . . one that's worth it.

At dinner parties, the taboo topics are religion and politics for good reason. Everyone has opinions, often divergent, about these issues. So hosts pray that people will keep the conversation to agreeable yet stimulating subjects. The minute a guest starts talking about the latest political scandal, watch what happens.

And the same thing goes for spiritual teachers, writers, and healers. You're crossing into taboo areas, since spirituality is so closely akin to religion. So this profession requires boldness, because you'll be stating convictions that others may not accept.

Can you handle it? Yes, of course you can. Remember, as I said earlier: There's never been any historical figure who was universally accepted by everyone. Anyone who's made a difference in this world has had detractors.

If you have a scrappy side to you, you may even enjoy debates with others. Yet, most spiritual teachers and healers are highly sensitive to—and even phobic about—conflict. Besides, it's impossible to convert anyone to your way of thinking with an angry tone. And I'm pretty sure that, like me, you're not interested in converting people anyway.

The best way to teach is to demonstrate your principles in your own life. *Live* as a role model of everything you're teaching. Walk your talk. I've done this by practicing a healthful, vegan, sober lifestyle for years . . . since that's what I believe in and teach.

The wonderful side benefits of walking your talk are that your self-esteem and confidence will stay high, because you know you're living by your principles.

In addition, the spirit world can plainly see which teachers and healers have the high vibration that accompanies right living. As part of your spiritual marketing team, they'll send clients your way if they believe in you. The best way to inspire their favor is by walking your talk.

Put the whole focus of your spiritual practice onto "How may I serve?" and don't even think about the material aspects—that is, making money or gaining public recognition. As you purify your motivation behind wanting to be a spiritual teacher or healer in the first place, you'll attract wonderful opportunities.

Spend time in meditation and prayer, visualizing cleansing light pouring through your mind, emotions, and body. Ask the light to elevate your motives and to move you past any financial or personal insecurities. Ask it to help set you on the firm platform of serving God through your livelihood.

Getting Your Message Out There

The spirit world will send you opportunities and clients as they learn that you're a teacher and healer who walks her talk and who's focused upon serving God. And you'll also receive additional Divine guidance to take action so that people know about your services.

Marketing a spiritual practice is much different from marketing a material commodity. Always keep in mind that your potential clients are highly psychic and sensitive, and they can smell insincerity and sales ploys.

Your best bet is to present your services to the public, and trust that the Law of Attraction will draw wonderful clients and opportunities to you . . . because it will!

People usually need to familiarize themselves with a spiritual healer or teacher before they're ready to book a session. So you'll want to present yourself in ways that allow them to get to know you, such as:

— **Articles in metaphysical magazines.** You know those free periodicals that you find on health-food-store racks? They're very popular. Write a 750-word article about your chosen topic, along with a one-paragraph bio of yourself (more on bios later), including your Website, e-mail address, or other contact details. Then submit this piece by e-mail to metaphysical-magazine editors.

You can find these magazines locally or through an Internet search engine like Google, by using key terms such as *New Age magazine, metaphysical magazine,* or *mind-body-spirit periodical.*

These small magazines don't pay their writers, but you *do* reap the reward of having your work published and your name being publicized, as well as the opportunity to reach many readers simultaneously.

— **Blogs and V-blogs.** In addition to writing articles for magazines, you can make an impact by writing web logs, or *blogs,* on your own Website or on a networking site such as Facebook. Video blogs or V-blogs are another option, where you upload film clips of yourself discussing various topics. And short blogs on sites like Twitter are popular ways to connect your teachings with other people.

— **Speeches and workshops.** When I first began work as a private-practice counselor specializing in treating eating disorders, I presented free talks at local health clubs and service organizations. These speeches promoted my ideas and my private practice. Three to four audience members would usually sign up as clients following each speech.

We'll discuss speaking in greater depth in the next chapter of this book.

— **Word of mouth.** All it takes is giving one great speech, healing session, or psychic reading, and everyone will know about you and your work. Word of mouth can be a powerful supporter of businesses because people trust their friends' opinions and feedback.

When I initially opened my private practice giving angel readings, I wasn't well known at all. One of my first clients was a woman who was big in the Alcoholics Anonymous 12-step program. Everyone knew her, it seemed. And when she really liked the reading that I gave her, she told everyone . . . and all of those friends and associates of hers booked sessions with me. Practically my whole private practice came from reading for that one lady, one time.

— **Prayers.** I've had powerful results by praying: *"I ask that everyone who would receive blessings by coming to my workshop be guided to attend and enroll today. I ask that they be supplied with the time, money, transportation, babysitting services, and anything else they need in order to attend."*

Attendees at my workshops regularly tell me amazing stories of how they just "happened" to find out about my seminar, and how they "coincidentally" got enough time or money to attend. By the way, feel free to rewrite the prayer for whatever service you're offering (healing sessions, arts enrichment, or what have you).

All of the above will help increase awareness of your spiritual practice, as well as give you valuable experience in feeling comfortable being in the public eye. So please keep it up. Sometimes it takes people several times seeing your face and reading your words in magazines and blogs before they're ready to book that appointment with you.

Your Bio

You'll need to create a biography about yourself to put in your articles, blogs, and pamphlets. Most lightworkers are shy about tooting their own horn or saying nice things about themselves, so you may want to ask a trusted friend for help with this.

Your bio needs to be written in the "third-person voice," which means it's as if another person is talking about you. So instead of "I have been practicing metaphysics since childhood," your bio would say: "Mary Smith has been practicing metaphysics since childhood."

In spirituality, the most important qualities that people tend to look for are relevant life experiences. In these fields, mystical encounters seem to hold more value than educational pursuits.

So if you've had any of the following types of life experiences, put them toward the top of your bio:

- You had a near-death experience or a brush with death, especially with a miraculous rescue involved.
- You've been talking with angels, fairies, departed people, and so on since childhood.
- You come from a family of psychics.
- You "escaped" from a job you disliked and are now employed in the field of your dreams.
- You manifested a soul-mate relationship that has lasted enough years for it to be considered a solid partnership.

In addition, be sure to include any rags-to-riches manifestation stories or profound mystical experiences.

Next in your bio would come spiritual schooling you've engaged in, such as studying meditation techniques. (Mention the name of your teacher if he or she is well known, or specify if your education was in a famous spiritual power place.)

After that, list any publications you've written or are working on. It's common practice for people to refer to their books in progress in this way: "Mary Smith is the author of the forthcoming book *How to Live a Life of Joy.*" Notice the word *forthcoming,* indicating that the manuscript is not yet published, but will be one day because you're in the process of writing it—which is a great affirmation, if you think about it.

Finally, list your relevant education and other work that supports your current career as a spiritual teacher or healer. For instance, "Mary Smith worked as a registered nurse at St. Jude Hospital in . . ." would be highly relevant to your current practice as a spiritual healer.

The best length for your bio is between two and four paragraphs. Be sure to include a sentence about your personality, such as "Mary Smith is a warm, entertaining, and inspiring speaker." (Your friends can help you write this, because they'll be happy to say kind things about you.)

Please don't worry: Your bio isn't an ego device. It's an information sheet to help people become familiar with you and your services. As long as you keep it real and warm, your intended clients will respond positively.

Entrepreneurship and Self-Employment

For many lightworkers, this is our first lifetime as a self-employed entrepreneur. As I mentioned in the last chapter, most of us spent previous lives being fully supported in communal living situations as monks, priestesses, nuns, scribes, servants, and such.

So if the idea of eking out a living repels you, you're not alone. In these other lifetimes, there was no concept of "separate property." No one (except for maybe royal families) had individual savings accounts. All your material needs were provided for automatically.

It's part of your personal spiritual growth to learn how to take care of yourself independently. You're here partially to learn how to ask for the fulfillment of your needs and to perform services in exchange. And the beautiful bottom line is that your services provide enjoyment and blessings for you and others. No more suffering . . . that's *so* last lifetime!

If self-employment is new to you, here are some of the qualities that it entails:

- **Self-discipline:** This refers to your ability to maintain a steady work schedule, without needing a boss to motivate you. This is the main reason why your profession must be built on a topic you're passionate about, because that passion will give you the drive and motivation to work instead of playing Internet games.

- **Jack- or Jill-of-all-trades:** As an entrepreneur, you get to make executive decisions one minute, and then take out the trash and sweep the floor the next.

- **Focus:** If you're working from your home, this is a doubly challenging part of your job. For example, you'll need to say *no* to neighbors who pop in for coffee and a chat just because you're around during the day (unless you're really good at balancing break time with work time).

- **Tenacity:** This means sticking to your dreams and intentions, even in the face of seeming rejection or delays.

- **Creativity and flexibility:** Sometimes your original route may need *re*routing.

- **Go for it–ness:** The angels once told me that the reason I get all kinds of cool opportunities is my penchant for saying *yes*. They know they can count on me to step up . . . and you can do the same.

- **Being able to pay your own taxes:** As an employee, you usually have your taxes withheld from each paycheck. As an entrepreneur, you'll need to calculate and plan for your taxes yourself. On the other hand, owning a business yields many opportunities for legal deductions (check with your local accountant for a complete list).

It's understandable if the preceding traits intimidate you. After all, the qualities that make you a sensitive healer or teacher are usually the polar opposite of the skills you need as a businessperson. To be a sensitive, psychic, or artist *and* an entrepreneur requires you to work out of both hemispheres of your brain.

One highly recommended option is to ease into self-employment by starting part-time in your healing and teaching profession while keeping your day job. This offers several benefits:

1. First, you never want to open a business with any kind of desperate need to make money. Sensitive New Age clients can feel desperation, which turns them off to you and your business, because it feels like you want something from them—a "taking" type of energy. Your clients need you to give to them, rather than placing energetic pressure on them to be your source of income.

So if you stay at your regular job for a steady paycheck, then you'll be able to approach your new profession with an abundance mentality that will attract a steady stream of clients and other forms of success.

2. You'll also be better able to withstand your day job if you have the pleasurable outlet of your new profession to look forward to during your off-hours. It will be your light at the end of the tunnel.

3. Then as your spiritually based business expands, you can either cut back your day job to a part-time position . . . or quit completely. You'll love the feeling of freedom when that day occurs.

Every position that you've held has yielded valuable skills and lessons, and no job is ever wasted. Treat your day job with gratitude for what it provides for you, and your loving energy toward it will help ease any tensions you may have experienced there.

I highly recommend that you frequently visualize and affirm success in your chosen profession. Your visions and words play a large role in determining the outcome of your new business.

Please remember:

Joy attracts clients.

Worry repels clients.

Give any anxiety to God through prayer, and put your whole focus upon "How may I serve?" Trust that as you give, the universe *must* give back to you in balance. Your only job is to be open to receiving, without worry or guilt.

CHAPTER 16

You Are a Professional Speaker

Whether you're a healer, artist, writer, or teacher, giving speeches is a wonderful way to spread healing energy, light, and love. You'll reach many people simultaneously, which enables you to make an even bigger difference in the world. . . .

"But How Do I Get Started?"

I wondered the same thing when I got the intuitive guidance to give speeches years ago. I was nervous about my skills as a speaker, as well as my qualifications for delivering the information. Yet the universe kept putting me in positions where I *had* to give lectures, as several jobs I held in the counseling field required me to teach publicly.

And it wasn't easy. One of my first such positions involved standing in front of a class and talking about alcoholism recovery to people who'd gotten tickets for drunk driving. They were at my class because of court orders, and they weren't happy about it.

Most of the students wore sunglasses and had their arms folded while I was teaching. Talk about a hostile audience! Well, at least it made me resilient with respect to that sort of thing so that I'm not frightened by potential critics in my present-day audiences. As I've said, *every* job yields valuable lessons.

It did help that I'd been in front of audiences since adolescence when I played guitar in several bands throughout San Diego County—although it's different when you can "hide" behind an instrument and your audience is largely intoxicated. When you speak to New Age audiences, there's no hiding . . . they can see everything in your aura and body language, as plain as day.

So I took several courses on public speaking, something that was really helpful. I enrolled in them at my local community college and at the extension program through UCLA. A couple of my publishers also paid for my training with media coaches. Every teacher and class yielded new insights and experiences.

Since surveys show that public speaking is a universal fear among people, these courses can give you confidence and courage. Except that I disagree with the old standby that you can reduce nervousness by picturing audience members in their underwear. That doesn't work at all. Instead, my nerves were allayed by . . .

1. Prayer

When Hay House booked me as the opening speaker for Louise Hay, Christiane Northrup, and Susan Jeffers during their "Empowering Women" tour back in the early '90s, and I peeked from behind the curtain at the size of the audience during our first stop, I began shaking with nervousness. I mean, my legs were wobbling!

So I went into a small room, closed the door, dropped to my knees, and prayed for help. I was due to go onstage in just a few minutes, and my voice was quivering! My personal miracle happened when I was guided to visualize myself surrounded by legions of loving and protective angels. As soon as I did so, my body relaxed. I got onstage, and as soon as I began speaking, the enthusiastic Detroit audience began to applaud. Thank You, God! Thank you, Detroit!

2. Blessing, Not Impressing

For some reason, I was very nervous one night before giving a speech to a large audience. So I went backstage and meditated. Soon, I clearly felt the presence of the healing angel, Raphael. In my mind, I heard him counsel me: *"Don't worry about impressing the audience. Instead, put your whole focus upon blessing them."*

Raphael was right! I *had* been worried about whether the audience would like me or my message; in other words, I was focused on *impressing* them. That was clearly coming from my ego. And since, as I've emphasized, the ego isn't psychic at all (being fear based), I would have given an *un*impressive workshop if I hadn't shifted my focus.

The ego is all about "me": *What if people don't like me? What if I can't do it? What if I mess up?* and other questions revolving around "me," "I," and "myself." With this sort of focus, a person is bound to stumble, making any fears come true.

The higher self, in contrast, is 100 percent psychic because it's pure love . . . which is one with everybody and everything. So your higher self communicates with a super-clear connection. Your readings are accurate, your healings are effective, and your speeches are articulate when you come from your higher self.

And you shift to this part of you by focusing upon serving "thou," or the audience who is one with you. In other words, your intention is to bless rather than impress.

3. Letting Go and Letting God

God is in charge of all spiritually based work. So it's important to open your mind and heart and allow the Creator's love to stream through you as you give that speech.

Sure, it's a good idea to have a basic outline of the contents, including opening and closing remarks. However, be flexible and open to Divine inspiration.

You'll get feelings about your audience's needs, so adjust your topic accordingly as your intuition directs. The same principle applies when responding to audience questions: Let the answers stream through you. As long as they're purely loving and kind, you can be certain they're Divine.

The Audience Members

The vast majority of people who attend spiritual workshops are kind and considerate, so you'll no doubt have a wonderful audience to work with. There's a real high from connecting with a group of love-minded lightworkers in a workshop setting, and you'll most likely enjoy giving spiritual seminars.

You may have one or two audience members, though, who pose issues for you and the other attendees. Here's how to deal with these situations:

1. The Co-teachers

These are audience members who want to help "co-teach" the class. They interrupt you to tell you their opinions or stories. While you'll want to encourage audience-sharing, these individuals are focused on impressing you and the other attendees, so they're not sharing in the sense of lovingly giving. They're actually *taking* . . . taking time away from *you* delivering your speech.

I can't emphasize enough how important it is for you to take charge of this situation. *Do not* give away your power to audience members, no matter how intimidating they or the circumstances are.

Your audience will become annoyed at both the Co-teacher *and* you if you don't assume control of the situation. After all, they spent time and money to hear *you* talk, not the other person.

You can say with warmth to the Co-teacher, "Wow, you seem to know a lot about this topic. However, if we all start to swap stories now, we'll get way off on tangents. So for the moment, I need to get back to the here-and-now with this topic and seminar." This acknowledges the individual's need for approval and usually helps him or her relax and listen to *you* talk.

2. The Hecklers

These are people who typically want to argue about religion. They'll demand to know why you haven't used the name God or Jesus 100 times in your speech.

The best way I've found to defuse the situation is to say with sincere compassion to the Heckler: "Oh, you seem to be very angry. I will pray for you to find your peace." After all, this person isn't at peace or he or she wouldn't be heckling you.

If the person wants to swap biblical quotes, beware. I've read the Bible many times, and I can "thump" the Good Book with the

best of them. But it's always a no-win situation. No one's mind is ever changed, and the audience becomes upset by the combative energy. Better to tell the Heckler: "This is fascinating, and I'd love to talk with you privately after the speech, because we're here to focus upon [name of topic] right now."

It's also important to have a set question-and-answer time for the audience. Let people know up front that you'll be responding to questions during a specific portion of your talk. As they raise their hands, you can say, "Oh, I'm happy to take questions in just a little while." Encourage audience members to write their questions down so they won't forget to ask them later.

As the speaker, you're the host of the event. So you'll need to extend the courtesy of beginning on time, taking breaks as needed, keeping the seminar focused on the topic, and ending the event according to schedule.

Where to Speak

The venues that are open for spiritual classes are endless, because all that's required are you and an audience. However, it's best to have standards for your speaking site—specifically, that it be a quiet and private location. After all, you'll likely be praying or meditating at some point. The last thing you want to hear is outside noise.

I once gave a speech in a hotel ballroom with an air wall dividing my room from another event, which turned out to be a church choir practice. And while their music was spectacular, we couldn't hear anything else in my workshop. Another time, I held an event in a room that had a wedding reception right below it . . . complete with banging drums.

But the ultimate experience was when I presented a seminar on the same day that a Harley-Davidson convention was being held next door. All day long the loud revving of engines reverberated into the room where I was holding meditations. But somehow we got through the event.

So these days, I check to see what other concurrent activities are scheduled before I'll agree to speak in a room.

Before you approach a venue to book your speech, you'll want to have at least three solid topics in mind, along with a one-paragraph description of each. Make your topics and descriptions "benefits oriented" so that your potential audience members will know what they'll gain by attending your talk.

For example:

Stress Management for Spiritually Minded People

> In this entertaining talk by Mary Smith, a professional healer, you'll learn the three ways to instantly calm yourself. You'll understand how to boost your immune system through simple processes that you can conduct at work, while driving, or in the midst of a busy day. Mary will guide you and the rest of the audience through a soothing meditation designed to bring healing energy into your mind and body. Mary will help you go from stressed . . . to blessed!

Offer three to four such titles and descriptions, along with your bio, on a pamphlet or in a letter; and contact the owners or event coordinators of the following venues:

Bookstores

Bookstores are in dire need of customers and financial support. They love to host events because these bring customers in the door. It's best to approach the owner of the store if it's locally owned, or the event coordinator if it's a chain bookstore. You can talk to this person on the phone, by e-mail, or in person.

— **Chain bookstores.** The large chains, although corporate run, often have genuine book lovers managing their individual stores. They're often very open to holding events such as book study groups, which is a wonderful way for you to gain experience and confidence as a speaker, as you sit in a circle with others and facilitate a discussion about your favorite book.

In addition, if you've been published—your inclusion as a story contributor in someone else's work qualifies—the store will be thrilled to have you speak about the book and sign it afterward.

Usually, chain bookstores offer free events, so you won't make money speaking there. However, you will gain valuable experience and potentially meet people who may set up appointments with you.

— **Metaphysical/New Age bookstores.** These charming Mom-and-Pop stores desperately need customers. Your seminar's revenue can help them stay in business.

In general, New Age bookstores charge money for their events, and you will receive a percentage of the ticket sales. The store knows the best price to charge, so do trust them with this decision. Then they'll likely ask you to split the revenue either 50-50 or a similar percentage. Do define your terms if they are taking expenses out of the revenue before paying you (gross versus net).

New Age bookstores love to host events that highlight the products they sell. These can include:

1. *Demonstrating a product:* Many of the Angel Therapists® who have taken my classes on working with oracle cards give bookstore presentations of how to use them. Everyone wins with these demonstrations: the clients love getting free mini-readings; the bookstore appreciates the increased customer foot traffic; and the Angel Therapists benefit from public-speaking experience, clients who book full appointments with them, and opportunities that accompany this. These are usually free, unpaid events.

2. *Speaking about a product:* Do you have a favorite book you'd like to tell the world about? The bookstore will be grateful for your speech featuring a book they sell. These are also usually free, unpaid events.

3. *Healing or support circle:* This is an event held on a regular basis. It can include an "angel healing circle," in which people gather in a circle and you lead prayers and meditations, or a support circle for a specific purpose such as "manifestation" or "grief recovery." These events are usually conducted on a donation basis.

4. *Seminars:* A seminar (also called a "speech") is a paid event in which you do most of the talking.

5. *Workshops:* A workshop is a longer experiential event in which you lead the audience through exercises (such as learning how to read oracle cards, give psychic readings, conduct energy healings, and so forth). These events usually charge a higher ticket price than a seminar/speech.

Churches and Temples

Places of worship have bills to pay, just like for-profit businesses. Their buildings often stand empty during non–service times; yet their electricity, phone lines, and mortgages must be paid for.

As such, they're grateful to host spiritual events to bring in new revenue, to offer services to their congregation and community, and to attract new members. They especially like to host guest speakers for events following a particular service (usually with a potluck lunch first and then your talk afterward).

Approach churches and temples by presenting the event coordinator with your flyer or letter listing your topics, descriptions of your talks, and your bio. You can hand-deliver, mail, or e-mail this material. Be sure to include your contact details!

Your material will be filed away until the next church/temple board meeting, where all prospective speakers are reviewed and voted upon. When you're approved, you'll be contacted to discuss dates and details.

Churches/temples host speakers in two ways:

1. You can rent their congregation hall for a nominal fee, around $50 an hour. This includes a staff member who will unlock and lock the doors and provide basic audio services such as a microphone and PA system.

2. You can coproduce the event with the church/temple. In this scenario, you don't pay anything up front for the room. But on the back end you'll split the ticket sales with the organization. They may want to collect the ticket money for the event, or they may ask you to do so.

In my experience, it's much better to use Option 2 and co-produce the event with the church/temple. They'll have an additional incentive to promote more attendees at your event because they're getting a percentage of each ticket. So, they'll publish articles about your talk in their member newsletter, create and post flyers about it on their bulletin board, and even invite you to discuss it during their service.

If you're invited to the pulpit to talk about your event, please say *yes*. Although it can be intimidating to stand in front of a congregation during their service, you can reach them in a whole new way. Just speak from your heart and briefly give them nuggets of wisdom that relate to what you're offering. Don't "sell" your event—just share—and trust that those who are guided will attend.

There are small, medium-sized, and large churches and temples. In my experience, the small and medium-sized places of worship are very open to new speakers. The large congregations usually only host famous speakers, so put that on your manifestation list. You can distinguish which churches/temples are small or medium sized by the number of services they offer each week. The mega churches/temples usually offer three or more weekly services, while the small houses of worship have one or two.

I've spoken at dozens of such places, but most commonly at Unity churches, which are nondenominational. You can find lists of locations at **unity.org**.

Mind-Body-Spirit Festivals and Fairs

For years I worked as a speaker for the Whole Life Expo, which was a touring group of spiritual speakers and vendors. We'd present expos two weekends a month in large U.S. cities such as Minneapolis and Austin. There were four or five famous keynote speakers who spoke one at a time. The lesser-known speakers spoke simultaneously three at once in small conference rooms.

Those who attended the expo were charged an admission fee, which entitled them to visit the free workshops and vendors' booths. Attendees paid extra for the keynote speeches by well-known people. The expo compensated speakers for their travel and lodging expenses, as well as for the talk. It was like being part of a traveling circus, because we all toured together for several years.

These types of expos, festivals, and fairs are wonderful starting points for spiritual teachers. They're held worldwide. The best way to find these events is through an Internet search engine using terms such as *mind-body-spirit festival* or *New Age expo,* or by looking for advertisements in metaphysical magazines.

The event contact details are the same whether you want to rent a booth or apply as a speaker. Send in your bio, your presentation topics, and workshop descriptions . . . and of course, your own contact details.

Some festival organizers will suggest that you rent vendor space, in addition to giving a talk. Only do so if you feel strongly guided to, as having a booth is a much different energy from giving a talk. One option is to get together with other spiritual healers or teachers and operate a booth together. Many Angel Therapists attend festivals where they give angel readings. They decorate booths with angelically inspired decor and offer paid readings. Sometimes they even sell items there.

Some festivals pay their speakers, and some do not. It's on a case-by-case basis, so hold clear intentions about your needs and expectations before you contact the event organizer. I can tell you that some vendors make a profit; and others just cover their travel, lodging, and booth-rental fees.

Healing, Health, and Wellness Centers

These centers usually offer public workshops on a regular basis. Your talk may or may not be paid, so be clear about your intentions before applying to speak at a healing center.

Retreat Centers

These centers are usually associated with yoga retreats, where you're surrounded by natural beauty in rustic but comfortable settings. Some retreat centers, such as Kripalu and Omega in the U.S., pay their speakers a percentage of the event's income. And others want speakers to rent their facility and produce their own events.

Service Organizations

Local community-service organizations, such as Kiwanis, Rotary, and Soroptimist, are always in need of guest speakers at their monthly meetings. You could offer a welcome alternative to the local sanitation manager discussing his new processing plant. You'll need to tone down the woo-woo esoteric portion of your talk for this audience, though. Usually service organizations favor topics that involve practical life issues, such as stress management.

I spoke at dozens of service-organization meetings when I first became a public speaker. They don't pay you, but you do get a free "rubber-chicken lunch," which refers to the standard club meal they serve everyone at these meetings. They do allow you to sell products and advertise your services during your talk, if that's of interest to you. I would advise bringing your appointment book, as many members of the organization will want to schedule sessions with you.

Your local library or newspaper has lists of local service organizations, along with contact details for their event coordinators.

Support Groups

If you specialize in a healing topic that could benefit a local support group, such as a grief-recovery meeting, then you'll definitely want to contact them about presenting a talk. Usually, these groups are small and don't have the budget to pay for speakers, but you can feel good about helping others in this way.

Adult Learning Centers

The most famous of these centers is The Learning Annex, operating in the U.S. and Canada, which offers interesting lectures given by experts and authors.

Adult learning centers feature a wide range of class topics, including careers, relationships, fitness, and spirituality. They normally welcome spiritual teachers on their rosters, and they hold their classes in rented hotel conference rooms, so they're not technically "centers" in the sense of a permanent facility. If you type the phrase *adult learning center* into an Internet search engine, you'll find various ones throughout the world.

Most classes are held on weeknights. The centers pay you a percentage of the income received for your class (usually a very low one), and you cover your own travel and lodging expenses unless you're a prominent speaker. They provide one or two employees or volunteers to help you with on-site registration and other class logistics. They do allow you to sell your products and advertise your services at these events.

Television and Radio

You can also present your topic through media outlets such as radio, television, and the Internet.

I've been interviewed about angels on hundreds of radio and TV shows, nearly always with very positive results. Radio stations adore psychic readers, so if you give readings, you'll definitely want to let the media know. And local morning TV programs are always seeking colorful guests, which is how they define spiritual teachers and healers.

I've been interviewed on news broadcasts, rock-and-roll stations, health programs, spiritual shows, and everything in between. Although many of the interviewers joked about my name ("Did you make up your last name?" was a common question, and the answer is "No, that's my real name") and my topic, the listeners really heard my message.

For example, one woman was tuning in to me on the radio while driving to the doctor's office to have a serious health problem checked out. She heard me discuss the importance of free will and asking God and the angels for help. She realized that she *hadn't* asked God for help, so she did so right then. By the time she arrived at the doctor's office, the condition was gone.

I enjoy radio interviews because they can be conducted from the comfort of your own home via telephone, with no makeup or fancy clothing required! At one time I was doing five to seven of these interviews a day, which was way too many. I ended up burning out on the experience, so please learn from my error and practice moderation.

If you'd like to be interviewed over the airwaves in the U.S., the best way to get booked is to place an advertisement in *Radio-TV Interview Report* (**rtir.com**). This media magazine will help you create an ad, which will yield amazing results.

You don't get paid to be on television or radio unless you're a Screen Actors Guild or other union member. But the experience and exposure may be worth it to you anyway, as you can promote your services, Website, and products during the interview.

Internet Sites and Tele-classes

You can also teach from your home thanks to modern technology. For instance, I've taught a few classes in chat rooms on spirituality Websites. Moderators take audience questions and help keep the chat organized. If you're a good typist, this is a fun way to connect with people. After a while, you forget that you're typing and it seems like you're speaking in an auditorium. You usually don't get paid for a chat-room course, but it's a wonderful outlet for sharing your message and creating awareness about your services.

"Tele-classes" and "video chats" are other Internet-based speaking venues. These allow you to teach multiple people through your home phone using conference-call technology or your computer over Skype or other Internet phone connections. Students pay to get a phone number and access code, which links them into your call. Some tele-classes allow for callers to voice their questions, while others keep students' telephones muted. Almost always, a moderator is involved in handling the logistics.

You do get paid a percentage to teach tele-classes. If you work with a producer, he or she will likely save the mailing list generated by the class, so do keep that in mind before booking yourself as a teacher. I feel protective of my students' e-mail information, which is one reason why I don't offer tele-classes unless I really trust the producer. Or better yet, you can produce your own class as long as you have the ability to spread the word about it to enough people.

And you can also teach on YouTube or other video sites, which is something I greatly enjoy. You don't get paid for these postings on public sites (although YouTube is constantly bugging me to get involved with something called "revenue sharing" for my popular videos, which I refuse to do on principle). I love the immediacy of connection via videos as a teaching avenue.

Out-of-Town Speakers

There's an old adage that says: "The expert is always from out of town." This means that people value a visitor's opinion more than someone who lives locally. There's a perception that visiting speakers know more and have more exotic experiences than a "common" local. This holds true for professional speakers as well, and you may find that you have greater success speaking in venues that are out of your area.

If you enjoy traveling, then you'll love being a professional speaker. Many times you're able to deduct your travel costs as a business expense, so you can pair a speech with a visit to see your family (check with your tax advisor, of course).

Microphones

Once your talk is booked, the producer will ask what type of microphone you prefer. Although you may gulp at the idea of your voice being amplified, it's a necessity to ensure that everyone hears your message. After a while, you'll forget that the microphone is even there, and it will feel natural to you.

There are three basic types to choose from:

1. **Handheld wireless.** This is the best choice for speakers who want to move around the stage or room, especially if you plan to talk with audience members. Since these microphones are unidirectional, your voice is only amplified if you speak directly into

the top of the mike, so be sure to hold it up high and close to your mouth.

2. **Handheld wired.** As long as you don't mind being tethered to the stage by the cord attached to the microphone, this is a very efficient way to amplify your voice. Since the cord is awkward, you may want to put the microphone on a stand and speak to it from where you are. Keep in mind, though, that this will be visually boring for your audience. It's much more entertaining to see you walk around the stage a bit and—even better—out into the audience.

3. **Lavalier.** This is a wireless clip-on microphone that you usually put on your lapel or collar. Sometimes it goes over the head (think Madonna in concert). Most speakers and audiophiles say that lavaliers have a poor sound quality compared to handhelds. I agree. I find that I speak louder to make myself heard through a lavalier, which is strenuous when you're talking for hours. You also don't have the option of sharing the lavalier microphone with an audience member unless you unclip it or awkwardly bend over.

Podium and Notes

The role you fill as a spiritual teacher is to educate audience members about esoteric concepts in understandable ways. So when giving your speech, you'll want to avoid anything that could block you from connecting with the audience . . . and that includes speaking podiums.

If you stand behind a podium or sit at a table, the audience will only see your upper half. Hiding from your listeners is disconnecting. Let them see all of you so they can fully feel your presence. Remember, those who attend spiritual workshops tend to be highly sensitive and psychic people.

You'll also want your talk to be spontaneous, so please don't read from notes the entire time. How boring it is to watch the top of someone's head while he looks down and reads a speech! It's fine for you to sit during your talk, as long as you remain animated and energized through your voice and mannerisms.

Smile and make eye contact with the people in the room to let them know you're genuine. They'll hear your message on a deep level if they trust that you're for real.

Music

If you plan on leading your audience through a meditation, then you'll want some background music. This is something you'll have to organize as the workshop presenter.

Ask your venue if they have a CD player or iPod-docking capabilities that run through their sound system. If not, plan to bring your own high-quality music player. It's a good idea to bring one anyway, just in case there are any problems with your venue's in-house system. Arrive with your recording of gentle background music ready.

Live music is even better, and local musicians who are on the spiritual path are often happy to play at such workshops. They will usually ask for a flat fee, plus the ability to sell and promote their CDs. Work out ahead of time whether you'll feel comfortable with the musician gathering a mailing list from your audience members, because this topic may come up during the event.

Answering Audience Questions

As I discussed earlier, provide a set time to answer audience questions. Take charge if you're interrupted while you're in the middle of telling a story or making a point. Don't let audience

members' questions steer you off onto a tangent, or you'll annoy the other attendees. As people raise their hands (or worse, shout out their questions), politely but firmly let them know that you'll be taking questions during a specific portion of the workshop. And then stick to this promise.

When you do take questions, make sure that everyone in the audience can hear them. It's disconcerting to only pick up one side of a conversation, which is how it will feel to audience members if they can't hear what's being asked. You can repeat the question into your microphone to make sure that you've understood it and to help the audience hear it. Or you can provide a microphone for audience members or share yours with them. Just don't give your mike away to a talkative audience member or you'll never get it back!

Giving Audience Readings

If you're a healer, psychic, medium, or angel reader, you'll probably conduct public readings for your audience members. This isn't much different from doing them via telephone or in person, except that they will be much shorter and will be amplified. Make sure that the individual you're reading is standing up and has a microphone (or that you share one) so everyone can see and hear the interaction.

With smaller-sized workshops, I prefer to go out into the audience and stand next to the person I'm reading. That way, I can offer a comforting hug or hand on the shoulder if we bring up sensitive emotions. With larger audiences, this isn't always practical, so I ask trusted healers to be "microphone runners," because they'll have a calming presence while holding the mike for the person for whom I'm conducting a reading from the stage.

I've toured, traveled, and shared stages with many speakers. Some of them are still going strong, and some have faded into obscurity.

Nearly every public speaker feels a degree of nervousness when approaching the podium. It's human nature! Actually, it's sentient-creature nature, as studies have shown that other species have performance anxiety, too.

One ingenious study involved teaching cockroaches how to run a maze successfully. Then the scientists introduced an "audience" of roaches to watch their peers. As soon as there was an audience, the subjects forgot how to run it!

The scientists concluded that performance anxiety is hardwired into us. It stems from a form of split attention: part of us is focused on our performance, and part on the audience's reactions.

And while it *is* important to monitor your listeners' mood and behavior—if everyone begins coughing and wiggling at the same time, this is time to take a bathroom break, for instance—your focus needs to be on your mission, talk, healing, and guidance. Release concerns about whether people are judging you or liking you.

Focus upon blessing, not impressing, your audience . . . and everything will go well.

CHAPTER 17

You Are a Spiritual Healer

If you're *guided* to be a healer, then you already *are* one . . . you just need to add the professional component. Everyone is a healer in truth, because we're made in the image and likeness of God, Who is *the* healer. Some people express this nature more readily than others.

Take a moment to recall your healing experiences. In what ways have you helped restore yourself and others (including pets) to wellness? As you remember these incidents, give yourself credit for stepping up and being the conduit of Heavenly healing energy. This isn't ego accolades; it's accepting positive responsibility for taking Divinely guided actions. This is healthy!

Becoming a Healing Professional

Many people call my radio show on **HayHouseRadio.com**® to ask how to transition from dreaming about being a healer to actually making a living as one.

As we discussed earlier, this depends upon your temperament with respect to self-employment. You've got to be self-directed in order to be your own boss. If this isn't your strong point, then consider starting off part-time in the healing field. You definitely don't want to begin a practice with a need for money, because any sign of desperation will scare off potential clients.

Another option is to work for a healing center so that you have a guaranteed income, or at least have a steady influx of client referrals from your place of business.

If you want to be a healer, the best guidance is to *do healing work*. Perform healings every day. You can start off doing them for yourself, friends, family, and pets to help you gain experience and confidence. Ask the people you work on to give you testimonials, if possible.

The turning point between practicing your healing art and making the leap to professional status begins with you. You must make the clear decision—unreservedly—that you will now be compensated. Sure, you'll give occasional freebies as you're guided. But you now expect, and so you manifest, payment for your healing work. And so it is!

Spend time journaling and meditating upon this intention. You'll need to reframe any guilt (probably from former lifetimes) about charging money for spiritual work. Otherwise, you'll push business away or engage in unconscious self-sabotage.

Remember, as you allow yourself to be paid, you're able to spend more time conducting your work. Payment allows you to leave a meaningless job so that you can create a *meaningful* career bringing healing blessings to others.

Think of it this way: when you allow yourself to receive, you have more resources available to give to others.

To find an outlet for your work, pray daily for opportunities to help others. I love the Prayer of Saint Francis: "Lord, make me an instrument of Thy peace." Then notice people who enter your life . . . they may have been Heaven-sent to assist you with your healing practice. Notice, too, any Divine guidance urging you to take action.

Speaking about Healing

Giving talks about your work is a wonderful way to foster awareness about you, your practice, and your healing modality. Even if you don't think of yourself as—or don't want to be—a professional speaker, you can bring great healing to many people through speaking engagements.

Your options include:

- Talking about your preferred healing modality to audiences
- Demonstrating this modality on one or more audience members (or the entire audience, if possible)
- Teaching others how to conduct this type of healing

All of the guidance and suggestions in the previous chapter apply as well.

Writing about Healing

If you're guided to write, you may want to start with penning articles for metaphysical or healing magazines. Ideally, create and submit these articles monthly. This will build your confidence

and writing experience, as well as help the public familiarize themselves with you and your practice.

Perhaps you're guided to write a book about healing. If so, I'd highly recommend the experience, as it is life changing (as well as helpful for your career).

For potential book authors, let me suggest that you buy or borrow these essential reference guides:

- *How to Write a Book Proposal* by Michael Larson (Writer's Digest Books). Larson's book gives step-by-step guidance about how to put together a saleable proposal, which will earn you a publishing contract. I followed the advice and proposal model in Larson's book to become successfully published.

- *Writer's Market* (Writer's Digest Books; also available in CD format). This reference guide lists U.S. and foreign publishers according to their genre (the topic of books they publish), along with their contact and submission details. Be sure to have the most current copy of this publication, because last year's book has stale information.

- *Dan Poynter's Self-Publishing Manual* (Para Publishing). Make sure to get a recent edition of this publication, which is updated regularly. This book is considered to be the first and last word about the ins, outs, hows, and whys of self-publishing a book.

Do I Need a Manager or Literary Agent?

In a word, *no.*

Let's start with managers: I worked with a couple of them early in my career as a public speaker. The first one was wonderful, but she was very busy with her main client, so we parted ways as friends. The second manager was quite expensive, taking half of all my income. When I ended that relationship, he sued me to *continue* receiving half my income. That wasn't fun.

Although you may not need a manager, you probably will want some help with booking appointments or speaking engagements. This is especially true if you aren't naturally organized or business minded. Would your spouse, adult child, or best friend be willing to help for an agreed-upon fee? If not, then consider hiring a part-time student to assist you. Just avoid hiring people who are overambitious, grouchy, or addicted, or who have a sense of entitlement. They're not fun either, and they can take a lot more time than if you had no employees at all.

If the preceding list of folks doesn't seem feasible, then you'll need to manage your own appointments—which can be a wonderful personal-growth experience. Yes, being a healer or psychic is very right-brained and intuitive. But you can balance those skills with left-brained activities such as setting up appointments. Just be sure to ground yourself first to avoid double-booking clients.

As far as literary agents go, you can publish a book without one, unless you're approaching a publisher that absolutely requires an agent, such as Hay House*.

If you want to approach a literary agent for representation, then I'd recommend one of the Writer's Digest books, which list

---

**Note:* I don't have an agent, so please don't ask me for a referral. Nor do I have a special "in" with Hay House to get you published; believe me, I've tried. And I apologize that I honestly don't have time to read, critique, or endorse your manuscript. Please understand that if I read every manuscript sent to me, I wouldn't have time to write my own books.

agents according to their specialties. The books also show you the best ways to pitch to these people. My editor at Hay House once told me that they look for these qualities in potential authors and books that they're considering publishing:

1. A fresh approach or a new topic.

2. Impeccable grammar and spelling. Pay an editor to proofread your query letter or book proposal.

3. A proven track record of marketing yourself and your work, with a history of either giving speeches, making radio or television appearances, publishing articles, and/or creating a Website that attracts a lot of visitors.

If you and your book have the above qualities, then go for it! Approach a literary agent, and I'll join in your prayers that you get published. Perhaps I'll see you at an upcoming author event!

CHAPTER 18

Self-Care for Spiritual Teachers and Healers

As I've discussed throughout this book, I *know* that you're a giving person. It's part of your lightworker personality and global mission. And yet, as I've emphasized repeatedly, it's essential to balance all that giving with receiving. Otherwise you're like an automobile that's constantly driven at top speed without stopping to refuel.

Guidelines for Healing Work

Your purpose as a spiritual teacher and healer is a lifelong mission, and I want you to enjoy your work for many years. Here are some guidelines to ensure longevity:

1. Honor Your Body as the Temple That It Is

This is the most important suggestion I can give you. Doing this work can be physically challenging, especially if you're traveling as a public speaker. Taking good care of yourself will give you the energy and health you'll need to withstand the stress involved with your career (such as airports, living out of a suitcase, time constraints, performance pressures, media interviews, deadlines, and demanding audience members or event producers).

The top speakers who are still going strong are those who exercise daily; eat healthfully; and avoid alcohol, cigarettes, marijuana, and other chemicals.

The speakers whom I once worked with who abused their bodies with over-partying aren't doing the work anymore.

Stamina comes from fueling your body right. That means all of the commonsense principles that your guardian angels are likely talking to you about daily: getting enough sleep, detoxing, exercising, meditating, and so forth. Many spiritual teachers and healers eat diets high in organic fruits and vegetables and avoid highly processed foods. A lot of us are vegetarians or vegans, because we're sensitive to the energy contained in the meat of mistreated animals. The angels have also guided many of us to adopt a glucose- and lactose-free diet because of our bodies' sensitivities to these substances. *Believe* your angels, trust your body's signals, and follow their lifestyle guidance.

Plus, Heaven can help you reduce cravings for alcohol, unhealthful food, and so on if you'll ask for their guidance. Archangel Raphael, in particular, can heal away addictive urges. Just think his name and ask for his assistance. He says *yes* to everyone, even those who are new to working with angels.

2. Honor Your Boundaries with Your Clients

This is my second-most-important suggestion to you. Your clients will naturally become attached to you, and some will grow dependent. Do everything possible to discourage dependency. Don't allow your clients to put you on a pedestal, because you'll eventually fall off.

Your clients are your professional associates, so it can be unhealthy and unwise to socialize with them. If you do so, then they're no longer clients. In many cases, they'll expect free services from you, because you're now their friend.

Similarly, when you open your healing or psychic-reading service, your current friends and family may expect free sessions. This is fine when you're starting out and need the practice to build confidence or gather testimonials. Just clarify that your complimentary sessions are a temporary measure until you get off the ground.

Once you're in business, it's fine to give discounts to family and friends . . . but they still should pay *something.* That ensures an energy exchange and helps you with the expenses that accompany a private practice.

I also find that when we're emotionally close to people, we lose the necessary objectivity to give them an accurate psychic reading. We're too invested in wanting a certain outcome for them, so it's difficult to see (or deliver a message about) anything that's different from their desires. So it may not be the best idea to have family and friends as clients. Perhaps refer them to another healer, who can then refer *her* family members to *you.*

It's also frowned upon to date clients, as this creates ethical issues. Your clients trust you as an authority figure, so engaging in romantic or sexual relations with them is overstepping your bounds and an abuse of power, which can lead to hurt and disappointment. Better to avoid this in the first place.

If you find yourself developing feelings for a client, talk to a trusted, experienced peer. Strongly consider ending your sessions with this person, to avoid putting yourself in a compromising position that you may later regret. Or end the client-healer relationship, let some time pass, and only *then* explore having a nonprofessional relationship with the person . . . exercising great caution with everyone's feelings.

Keep your clients as clients, and only see or talk with them during allotted appointments. *Do not* give them your home phone or personal cell number or your private e-mail address. Keep your personal and professional lives separate! If a client calls to book an appointment and wants to ask a couple of psychic-reading questions at that time, avoid the temptation to give free samples. Otherwise, you'll teach your clients to expect bonus readings whenever they call. From the start, if you model healthy boundaries for your clients, they'll respect you more.

3. Watch Your Ego

Your clients and audience members will lavish you with praise about how wonderful and special you are. Be careful about accepting compliments, and take them with a grain of salt! The writer Charles Clark Munn said it best when he quipped: "Compliments are like perfume, to be inhaled, not swallowed."

When people praise you, they're doing so as a form of affection. Most compliments are trumped-up versions of the sincere feelings that these admirers genuinely have but don't know how to express. So most people overdo it with flattery.

If you take their words to heart, you risk going into your ego, which is what happens whenever you allow yourself to feel special. "Specialness" is a sign of feeling better than someone else, which is the basis of the belief in separation. And the thought of being separated from others and from God is the foundation of all

fear and guilt. It's healthier to take compliments in the spirit that we're *all* equally special and gifted.

Since compliments are a gift and it's important to allow yourself to receive, there are gracious ways to accept them and still stay out of your ego. For instance, smiling and saying "Thank you" is always appropriate. In your head, give the compliment to God, Who is the source of everything your client appreciates about *you.*

Please keep in mind that your ego is completely fear based, 100 percent *not* psychic, and *without* healing abilities. So if you allow yourself to swallow your clients' remarks, then you'll lose touch with the very skills that they complimented in the first place.

When you see healers and psychics advertising themselves as the "most gifted" or the "world's best psychic," run the other way. Those people have swallowed their compliments and are operating out of their egos' separation beliefs. And you don't want that same thing to happen to you.

4. Make Business Decisions Based on Guidance

Many healers open their private practices because of strong Divine guidance. Everything flows nicely because their actions have a nice, solid spiritual foundation.

But if financial worries set in, a healer's actions may be motivated by fear. She can no longer hear her inner guidance, so she takes fear-based courses of action. This will lead her practice into a whole other energy and direction.

5. Deal with Your Changing Relationships

If you think that becoming a professional spiritual teacher or healer will change your life, you're right. But it's not always in ways you'd expect.

One significant change concerns your relationships. Your new career gives others great insight into your beliefs. If you've kept your feelings private in the past, you may feel a little exposed . . . especially if your career path is met with teasing or resistance from your friends and family.

Or you may find that people express jealousy over your newfound happiness and success. Perhaps they worry that you're going to change so much that you'll leave them behind.

But the biggest life change will occur in your relationship with your own self. You'll begin to honor yourself more than ever, so you'll opt out of activities that seem harsh or "off center." This can be threatening to your family and friends, who are accustomed to hearing you say *yes* to everything in the past.

If possible, it's best to deal with these changes openly and honestly. If your family dynamics discourage candid discussions, then hold conversations with your loved ones' guardian angels to heal any divides or misunderstandings.

Ethical Considerations

As a spiritual healer and teacher, you'll gain the confidence of your clients, so some will reveal intimate personal information to you. Of course you'll honor your clients' privacy and not gossip about their lives. What they say is confidential, just as it would be with a doctor or attorney.

If you decide to relate a client's story in a book or article, you either need to get written permission from that person or you must scramble his or her personal details so that no one would recognize whom you're discussing. For example, make a male client into a female; and change the person's occupation, age, and city of residence. Write only the core nuggets of the story, to the degree that it will help others who read it.

Keep your promises to everyone, including your clients. Be punctual and thoughtful, kind, and considerate to everyone, including yourself.

If a client comes to you and mentions suicide, *be careful*. Err on the side of caution and bring in professionals to help. Don't try to play superman or superwoman with such a client. Your role is to call for emergency assistance and let experienced professionals do their job to save this person's life.

And please know your educational and licensing restrictions with respect to healing work. If you're not a doctor, nurse, or psychologist, please don't step into those areas with your client. Be very conservative when giving readings about medical conditions or marital relationships. Don't overstep your bounds.

It's a great idea to develop a business relationship with trusted medical and psychological personnel so that you can refer clients to them when your professional limits are tested. You can find spiritually minded health-care professionals through your local church, temple, or metaphysical center.

With each situation that arises in your spiritual healing practice, you'll be guided and supported. Stay in the present moment, do your best to listen to and follow your intuition, and give any worries about tomorrow to God.

Afterword

You *Are* a Spiritual Teacher and Healer!

Your dream of developing a spiritually based career is much more than an idle fantasy. It's a clear sign of your destiny and your soul's leanings.

If you follow your true path, you will see such a happy planet. So much needless anxiety comes from working at an unfulfilling job just for a paycheck. When you develop a meaningful career, in contrast, your whole life takes shape.

Know that you've been a spiritual teacher and healer for many lifetimes. You've certainly been one throughout *this* life, including as a child (just think back and you'll recall moments revealing your talents and interests).

Hold that clear identity for yourself and your actions will naturally follow. Daily investments of five minutes or more will open the doorways to your new life and future. It's here, waiting for you now!

What's the first step to take? You've *already* taken it by dreaming about your ideal career. Now, turn that into reality by listening—really *listening*—to the answer your higher self gives you when you ask the question: "What changes would you like to see me make in my life right now?"

Trust the answer that you get . . . and follow, one step at a time, the path of your life purpose. Enjoy!

— Doreen

Endnotes

Chapter 6

1. Stevenson, I. (1992). "A Series of Possibly Paranormal Recurrent Dreams." *Journal of Scientific Exploration,* Vol. 6, No. 3, pp. 282–289.

Chapter 9

1. West, D. J. (1960). "Visionary and Hallucinatory Experiences: A Comparative Appraisal." *International Journal of Parapsychology,* Vol. 2, No. 1, pp. 89–100.

2. Stevenson, I. (1983). "Do We Need a New Word to Supplement 'Hallucination'?" *The American Journal of Psychiatry,* Vol. 140, No. 12, pp. 1609–11.

3. Osis, K., and Haraldsson, E. (1997). *At the Hour of Death.* Third Edition (Norwalk, CT: Hastings House).

Appendix

Specialties of the Archangels

Ariel—connecting with nature, animals, and nature spirits (for example, fairies); manifesting your earthly material needs; guidance for a career or avocation in environmentalism or animal welfare.

Azrael—healing the bereaved; helping souls cross over; assisting grief counselors.

Chamuel—universal and personal peace; finding whatever you are seeking.

Gabriel—delivering important and clear messages; helping those who are messengers (teachers, writers, actors, and artists); assisting with all aspects of parenting, including conception, adoption, and birth.

Haniel—awakening and trusting your spiritual gifts of intuition and clairvoyance; releasing the old; support and healing for women's physical and emotional health issues.

Jeremiel—developing and understanding spiritual visions and clairvoyance; conducting a life review so you can make adjustments with respect to how you wish to live.

Jophiel—beautifying and uplifting your thoughts and feelings; clearing clutter out of your life.

Metatron—sacred geometry and esoteric healing work; working with the universal energies, including time management and "time warping"; helping highly sensitive people (especially the youths who are often referred to as *Indigos* or *Crystals*).

Michael—protection, courage, confidence, and safety; life-purpose guidance; fixing mechanical and electronic items.

Raguel—healing arguments or misunderstandings; bringing harmony to situations; attracting wonderful new friends.

Raphael—healing of people and animals; guiding healers in their education and practice; guidance and protection for travelers; connecting you with your soul mate.

Raziel—understanding the secrets of the universe; remembering and healing from past lives; understanding esoteric wisdom, such as dream interpretation.

Sandalphon—receiving and delivering prayers between God and humans; guidance and support for musicians.

Uriel—intellectual understanding; conversations; ideas, insights, and epiphanies; studying, school, and test taking; writing and speaking.

Zadkiel—helping students remember facts and figures for tests; healing painful memories; remembering your Divine spiritual origin and missions; choosing forgiveness.

Halo Colors of the Archangels

Ariel—pale pink

Azrael—creamy white

Chamuel—pale green

Gabriel—copper

Haniel—pale blue (moonlight)

Jeremiel—dark purple

Jophiel—dark pink

Metatron—violet and green

Michael—royal purple, royal blue, and gold

Raguel—pale blue

Raphael—emerald green

Raziel—rainbow colors

Sandalphon—turquoise

Uriel—yellow

Zadkiel—deep indigo blue

Crystals and Gemstones Associated with the Archangels

Ariel—rose quartz

Azrael—yellow calcite

Chamuel—fluorite

Gabriel—copper

Haniel—moonstone

Jeremiel—amethyst

Jophiel—rubellite or deep pink tourmaline

Metatron—watermelon tourmaline

Michael—sugilite

Raguel—aquamarine

Raphael—emerald or malachite

Raziel—clear quartz

Sandalphon—turquoise

Uriel—amber

Zadkiel—lapis lazuli

Astrological Signs Associated with the Archangels

Michael, Raphael, and Haniel—the overseers of all

Ariel—*Aries,* the light, carefree, happy spirit

Azrael—*Capricorn,* the healer concerned with mortality, transitions, and finality

Chamuel—*Taurus,* the persistent finder of what is being sought

Gabriel—*Cancer,* the nurturing and hardworking parent

Jeremiel—*Scorpio,* the truth teller who goes into shadows comfortably

Jophiel—*Libra,* the lover of beauty and orderliness

Metatron—*Virgo,* the hardworking, industrious, inventive, curious, serious perfectionist

Raguel—*Sagittarius,* the sociable peacekeeper

Raziel—*Leo,* the dramatic rainbow of colors and bright light

Sandalphon—*Pisces,* the artsy dreamer

Uriel—*Aquarius,* the thinker and analyzer

Zadkiel—*Gemini,* the sociable but studious multitasker

About the Author

Doreen Virtue holds B.A. and M.A. degrees in counseling psychology from Chapman University, a Ph.D. in counseling psychology from California Coast University, and an associate's degree from Antelope Valley College. She is a lifelong clairvoyant who works with the angelic realm.

Doreen is the author of *Healing with the Angels, How to Hear Your Angels, Messages from Your Angels, Archangels & Ascended Masters, Solomon's Angels,* and the *Archangel Oracle Cards,* among other works. Her products are available in most languages worldwide.

Doreen has appeared on *Oprah,* CNN, *The View,* and other television and radio programs. She writes regular columns for *Woman's World, Spheres,* and *Spirit & Destiny* magazines. For more information on Doreen and the workshops she presents, please visit: **www.AngelTherapy.com**.

You can listen to Doreen's live weekly radio show, and call her for a reading, by visiting **HayHouseRadio.com®**.

Hay House Titles of Related Interest

YOU CAN HEAL YOUR LIFE, the movie,
starring Louise L. Hay & Friends
(available as a 1-DVD program and an expanded 2-DVD set)
Watch the trailer at: **www.LouiseHayMovie.com**

THE SHIFT, the movie,
starring Dr. Wayne W. Dyer
(available as a 1-DVD program and an expanded 2-DVD set)
Watch the trailer at: **www.DyerMovie.com**

THE ART OF EXTREME SELF-CARE: Transform Your Life One Month at a Time, by Cheryl Richardson

COLORS & NUMBERS: Your Personal Guide to Positive Vibrations in Daily Life, by Louise L. Hay

GREEN MADE EASY: The Everyday Guide for Transitioning to a Green Lifestyle, by Chris Prelitz

INSPIRED DESTINY: Living a Fulfilling and Purposeful Life, by Dr. John F. Demartini

LOYALTY TO YOUR SOUL: The Heart of Spiritual Psychology, by H. Ronald Hulnick, Ph.D., and Mary R. Hulnick, Ph.D.

THE MAP: Finding the Magic and Meaning in the Story of Your Life, by Colette Baron-Reid

THE SURVIVAL OF THE SOUL, by Lisa Williams

All of the above are available at your local bookstore,
or may be ordered by contacting Hay House (see next page).

We hope you enjoyed this Hay House book. If you'd like to receive our online catalog featuring additional information on Hay House books and products, or if you'd like to find out more about the Hay Foundation, please contact:

Hay House, Inc., P.O. Box 5100, Carlsbad, CA 92018-5100
(760) 431-7695 or (800) 654-5126
(760) 431-6948 (fax) or (800) 650-5115 (fax)
www.hayhouse.com® • www.hayfoundation.org

Published and distributed in Australia by: Hay House Australia Pty. Ltd., 18/36 Ralph St., Alexandria NSW 2015 • *Phone:* 612-9669-4299 • *Fax:* 612-9669-4144 www.hayhouse.com.au

Published and distributed in the United Kingdom by: Hay House UK, Ltd., 292B Kensal Rd., London W10 5BE • *Phone:* 44-20-8962-1230 • *Fax:* 44-20-8962-1239 www.hayhouse.co.uk

Published and distributed in the Republic of South Africa by: Hay House SA (Pty), Ltd., P.O. Box 990, Witkoppen 2068 • *Phone/Fax:* 27-11-467-8904 www.hayhouse.co.za

Published in India by: Hay House Publishers India, Muskaan Complex, Plot No. 3, B-2, Vasant Kunj, New Delhi 110 070 • *Phone:* 91-11-4176-1620 • *Fax:* 91-11-4176-1630 www.hayhouse.co.in

Distributed in Canada by: Raincoast, 9050 Shaughnessy St., Vancouver, B.C. V6P 6E5 *Phone:* (604) 323-7100 • *Fax:* (604) 323-2600 • www.raincoast.com